WEEKEND QUILT PROJECTS

Publications International, Ltd.

Contributing Designers:

Judy Gelzinis Donovan has been creating quilts and wearable art since 1981. Her work has appeared in many art shows and national publications, including *Quilting Quarterly* and *International Quilt Festival*. She is a member of the American Quilter's Society and the National Quilting Association. Her design appears on page 94.

Joanna E. Evans is a quilter and freelance writer who serves as Vice President of the Bloomington Quilters Guild and is a member of the Indiana State Quilters Guild. One of her designs appears in *America's Best Quilting Projects: Scrap Quilts,* and she has written patterns for *Traditional Quiltworks* and *Quilting Today*. Her designs appear on pages 36 and 124.

Cheryl Fall is the author of *Country Quilts & Soft Furnishings, Seasonal Quilting: A Year in Stitches, Happy Quilts, Treasury of Quilting Patterns,* and *Hung by the Chimney with Care: Quilted Stockings.* She is a regular contributor to the magazines *Creative Quilting* and *Quick and Easy Quilting,* among others. She designs for a number of manufacturers, including Coats & Clark. Her designs appear on pages 65 and 88.

Lynne Farris is a member of the Society of Craft Designers, and her designs have appeared in *Crafts, McCall's Quilting,* and *Creative Sewing.* She is currently writing a book on soft sculpture. She also designs costumes for promotional characters, such as the mascot for the Atlanta Hawks basketball team. Her designs appear on pages 62, 74, 99, 107, and 141.

Judith Sandstrom is a member of the Society of Craft Designers and the American Quilter's Society. Her original quilt designs have appeared in *Quilt World, Stitch n' Sew Quilts, Quilt Craft,* and *Quick & Easy Quilting.* Her quilts appeared in the book *Great American Quilts 1995* and on the television show *Creative Living with Crafts.* Her designs appear on pages 24, 82, 102, and 112.

Vicki Jackson Schweitzer has taught quilting at Northern Kentucky University for the past 18 years. She teaches at quilt shops and seminars across the country and serves as President of the Licking Valley Quilters Guild. She is a member of the National Quilting Association, and she self-publishes her own books and patterns. Her designs appear on pages 40, 58, 78, and 128.

Retta Warehime has taught piecing for over 16 years at quilt shops all over the country and at community colleges. She designs and markets her own patterns and has published four books: *Seasoned with Quilts, Ohio Evenings, Snowmen Medley,* and *Fast, Fun and Fabulous Quilts.* She also created designs for *Quilted for Christmas 11.* Her designs appear on pages 30, 47, 116, 132, 146, 153, and 162.

Contributing Writer: Joanna E. Evans

Contributing Consultant: Judith Sandstrom

Illustrators: Yoshi Miyake and Sally Schaedler

Photography: Chris Cassidy Photography

Photo Stylist: Danita Wiecek

Location: Sweet Basil Hill Farm Bed & Breakfast, represented by B&B MidWest Reservations

Louis Weber, C.E.O.
Publications International, Ltd.
7373 North Cicero Avenue
Lincolnwood, Illinois 60646

Permission is never granted for commercial purposes.

Manufactured in U.S.A.

8 7 6 5 4 3 2 1

ISBN 0-7853-1299-4

Library of Congress Catalog Card Number: 95-72808

CONTENTS

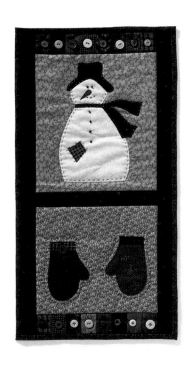

INTRODUCTION

Quilting is a centuries-old craft that originated with thrifty people who did not want to waste scraps of fabric and outgrown clothing. Over the years, quilters learned to turn their warm, practical creations into

real works of art. Nowadays, with the help of modern techniques and technology, you can create a beautiful quilt in just a weekend—even if you're not an experienced quilter.

If you have not done much quilting, read the information that follows. This section will help you familiarize yourself with quilting techniques, both modern and old-fashioned, and materials. You can use this basic knowledge to make the quilts in this book or to create your own original masterpieces. To help you choose the quilts that are right for your level of experience, each project is labeled as "easy," "moderate," or "difficult."

MATERIALS

FABRIC

In general, it is worth investing in the best materials you can afford. Many inexpensive fabrics are less likely to be colorfast. Avoid the regret that goes with choosing a fabric that isn't quite perfect because it is less expensive than the fabric you love.

Try to select only 100-percent cotton fabrics for the face and back of the quilt. Cotton is easy to cut, mark, sew, and press. It is also widely available. Fabrics that contain synthetics, such as polyester, are more difficult to handle and are more likely to pucker.

Top: Warm colors.
Bottom: Cool colors.

For the most part, you should select colors of one type—either bright or pastel—to use in one quilt. Consider using cool colors like purple, blue, and white or warm colors like yellow, orange, red, and off-white.

Sometimes a fabric that seems light by itself is very dark next to other fabrics. To avoid this, look at all the fabrics you plan to use through a red transparent report cover (available in most stationery stores). Do the fabrics you thought were dark *look* dark next to the ones you thought were light? Do you mix light and dark fabrics? Does this create the effect you are trying to achieve?

Use prints with a variety of scales or all with the same scale. That is, use large prints, medium prints, and small prints in the same quilt or use only large, medium, or small prints. If you use all small prints with one large-scale print, the large-scale print will probably look out of place.

Left: Large, medium, and small prints. Right: Three small prints.

When you have selected fabrics, buy a small amount of each (no more than ¼ yard). Cut out enough of each fabric to make up one block. Evaluate the block. Are you happy with all the fabrics and how they work together? Step back and look at the block from a distance. Does it still look good? This is the time to make changes to your fabric selection if necessary. Be sure you do it right away so the material is still in the store.

6

The backing fabric should be similar in fiber content and care to the fabrics used in the quilt top. Some wide cottons (90 and 108 inches) are sold specifically for quilt backings. They eliminate the need to piece the back.

As you work on quilts, it's a good idea to keep a scraps basket rather than discarding unused fabric. Some quilts call for very small amounts of fabric for appliqués. If you can find the right color among your scraps, you'll save yourself the trouble and waste of purchasing ⅛ yard of fabric for a much smaller piece.

BATTING

There are many types of batting to meet the needs of different projects. In general, use polyester batting with low or medium loft. For a puffier quilt, use high-loft batting, but consider tying the quilt, since this batting is difficult to quilt. Polyester is better if the quilt will be washed frequently. Cotton batting is preferred by some quilters for a very flat, traditional-looking quilt. Wool batting is a pleasure to quilt and makes a warm cover.

THREAD

It may seem tempting to use up old thread on a quilt. However, working with old, weak thread is frustrating because it tangles and knots—and working with high-quality, new thread is a joy. Consider buying 100-percent cotton thread or good long-staple polyester thread for piecing, appliqué, and machine quilting. Use monofilament nylon thread (.004mm or size 80) for freehand machine quilting. Cotton quilting thread is wonderful for hand quilting but should not be used for machine quilting because it is stiff and will tend to lie on the surface of the quilt.

For piecing by hand or by machine, select a neutral color thread that blends in with most of the fabrics in the quilt. For most projects, either khaki or gray thread works well. Use white thread for basting; do not risk using colored thread that may leave color behind. For appliqué, the thread should match the fabric that is being applied to the background. The color of quilting thread is a personal design choice. If you want your quilting to show up, use a contrasting thread color.

MATERIAL PREPARATION

PREWASHING

Always wash fabrics first. This will remove some of the chemicals added by the manufacturer and make it easier to quilt. Also, cotton fabric does shrink, and most of the shrinkage will occur during the first washing and drying. Be sure to use settings that are as hot as those you intend to use with the finished quilt.

Dark, intense colors, especially reds, tend to bleed or run. Wash these fabrics by themselves. If the water becomes colored, try soaking the fabric in a solution of three parts cold water to one part white wine vinegar. Rinse thoroughly. Wash again. If the fabric is still losing its color, discard the fabric and select another. It is not worth using a fabric that may ruin the other fabrics when the finished quilt is washed.

MAKING TEMPLATES

To make templates from full-size patterns, trace the pattern onto template plastic with a sharp pencil or a fine-tipped permanent pen. Use scissors to cut out the templates.

ENLARGING PATTERNS

Where pattern pieces are too big to be printed in this book, smaller versions are printed. Use a photocopy machine to enlarge them to the desired size or enlarge them by hand using the grid method.

Directions on the patterns will tell you the percentage for enlarging each pattern on a photocopier. If you must make a copy of a copy, turn the copy 90 degrees each time you place it on the machine. This minimizes possible distortions created by the copier.

To use the grid method, draw or buy paper with one-inch grid lines. Draw a grid over the pattern using the smaller measurement, then redraw the illustration from this book on the one-inch grid, matching square for square. To make templates, trace from the full-size pattern.

MARKING AND CUTTING FABRIC

To cut fabric the traditional way for piecing or appliqué, place the template on the wrong side of the fabric. The arrow on the template indicating the grain should be aligned with the straight grain or the crosswise grain of the fabric.

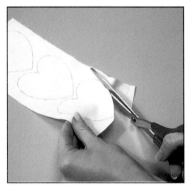

Trace around the template with a hard-lead pencil or a colored pencil designed for marking on fabric. Yellow or silver pencils generally show up well on dark fabrics. Never use a ball-point pen or other marking tool with ink that may run. If the template does not include a seam allowance, add one. Cut around each piece with sharp fabric scissors.

In many cases, it is faster and easier to cut fabric using a rotary cutter. This tool, which looks and works like a pizza cutter, must be used with a self-healing mat and a see-through ruler. Always employ the safety shield of the rotary cutter when it is not in use.

Fold the fabric in half lengthwise with the selvages together. Adjust one side until the fabric hangs straight. The line that is created by the fold is parallel to the fabric's straight of grain. Keeping this fold in place, lay the fabric on the mat. Place a see-through ruler on the fabric. Align a grid line on the ruler with the fold and trim the uneven edge. Apply steady, even pressure to the rotary cutter and to the ruler to keep them and the fabric from shifting. Do not let the cutter get farther away from you than the hand that is holding the ruler. Stop cutting and reposition your hand.

Reposition the ruler so that it covers the width of the strip to be cut and the trimmed edge is on the markings for the appropriate measurement on the ruler.

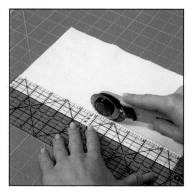

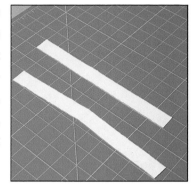

After cutting the strip, hold it up to make sure it is straight. If it is angled, refold the fabric and trim it again. Continue cutting strips, checking frequently that the strips are straight.

TOOL SELECTION

A sharp pair of scissors is essential for quilting. Ideally, set aside a pair of scissors to be used on fabric only. Paper and plastic quickly dull the cutting edges of scissors, so keep a separate pair for cutting out templates and other nonfabric items.

To cut fabric quickly and easily, invest in a rotary cutter, see-through ruler, and self-healing mat. These tools let you cut strips of fabric efficiently. If you become very involved with quilting, you may find that a collection of cutters, mats, and rulers of different sizes and shapes is valuable. A good starter set would include the large-size cutter, a mat at least 22 inches wide, and a 6×24-inch ruler.

Most fabrics can be marked with a hard-lead pencil. Mechanical pencils are worthwhile investments because they are always sharp. A special fabric eraser can help remove light pencil markings. Other handy marking tools include colored pencils designed for marking on fabric and a fine-tip permanent pen for signing your finished quilt. Soapstone pencils make a light mark that is easy to brush off, but they lose their sharp point quickly and must be sharpened often. Tailor's chalk or chalk wheels are helpful for marking quilting patterns just before you quilt. The chalk brushes off fabric easily. Disappearing ink pens may be tempting because they make a mark that is easy to see, but heating fabric that contains residue from the ink can create a permanent stain. Leaving a work in progress in a hot car or in a sunny window can cause this to happen. Consider banning this risky product from your quilting basket.

Traditionally, templates were made of scrap cardboard. Cardboard is satisfactory, although if a template is going to be used many times, template plastic is better because it does not wear down. Template plastic is available as plain white sheets or transparent sheets printed with a grid.

The needles used for hand piecing and hand appliqué are called sharps. For hand quilting, use betweens (quilting needles). Generally, start with a size 8 and work toward using a size 10 or 12. Use the smallest needle you can to make the smallest stitches.

Always use a sharp needle on your sewing machine; a dull needle will tend to skip stitches and snag the threads of your fabric, creating puckers. Use size 9/70 or 11/80 for piecing and appliqué and size 11/80 (in most cases) or 14/90 (for a thick quilt) for machine quilting.

Use fine, sharp straight pins (such as silk pins) for piecing and holding appliqué pieces in place before basting or stitching. Long quilter's pins are used to hold the three layers (top, batting, and backing) before they are basted together or quilted. Have a large box of safety pins (size 2) on hand for basting for machine quilting.

Quilting supplies: a) quilting hoop, b) self-healing mat, c) see-through ruler, d) rotary cutter, e) darning foot, f) even-feed walking foot, g) quilter's thimble, h) sharp, i) scissors, j) betweens, k) safety pins, and l) template plastic.

If you plan to quilt by hand, you need some way of holding the area you are stitching smooth. Some people do this successfully with their hands, but most quilters prefer to use a quilting hoop or quilting frame. Quilting hoops are portable and inexpensive. A small area of the quilt is surrounded by the hoop, which keeps the fabric taut. For large bed quilts, many quilters prefer to use a quilting frame, which supports the entire quilt, with large areas available for quilting at any given time. However, quilting frames are a significant investment and require space. Consider using quilting hoops until you feel the need to work on a quilting frame. All the projects in this book can be completed successfully with a hoop. Experiment with different styles to see what feels most comfortable.

You will need a handy steam iron and ironing board. To streamline your workflow, place the ironing board at right angles to the sewing table and raise it to the same height. This arrangement will allow you to press seams after they are stitched without getting up.

Quilts can, of course, be made entirely by hand. Today, however, many quilters do all their piecing—and some do all their quilting—by machine. The machine does not have to make lots of fancy stitches. It does need to stitch an accurate ¼-inch seam with an even tension.

PATCHWORK TECHNIQUES

Unless otherwise noted, all seam allowances for projects in this book will be ¼ inch.

Accuracy is important. A small error repeated in each block or, worse yet, in each seam, will become a large distortion. Before starting a large project, make a sample block and measure it. Is it the desired size? If not, figure out where the inaccuracy occurred. Are any seams a few threads too wide or narrow? Clip seams and restitch.

HAND PIECING

With right sides together, align fabric pattern pieces so that the ends of the seam match. (Use straight pins to check.) Pin the seam. Make sure the seam lines match exactly.

Cut a piece of thread approximately 18 inches long. Put the end that came off the spool of thread first through the eye of the needle. Knot the other end, using a quilter's knot.

To make a quilter's knot, wrap the end of the thread around the tip of the needle (wrapping from the base toward the point of the needle) three times. Then pull the needle through the wraps. Pull the knot down to the end.

Stitch from one end of the seam to the other, using a running stitch (about eight stitches per inch). For additional strength, backstitch at the beginning and end of each seam. Do not stitch across the seam allowance. In general, press the seam toward the darker fabric.

MACHINE PIECING

When machine piecing, set the sewing machine's stitch length to 10 to 12 stitches per inch (or between 2 and 3 on machines that do not use the stitches per inch measure). Stitch across the

seam allowance, along the seam line, and across the seam allowance at the far end of the seam. Do not backstitch.

Make sure the seam allowance is consistently ¼ inch. The presser foot on a few sewing machines is a true ¼ inch. Stitch a sample and measure the seam allowance. If you are off by just a hair on each piece you stitch, the errors will accumulate, and the end result may be distorted.

If your sewing machine does not have a mark or a ¼-inch-wide presser foot, place several layers of masking tape to act as a sewing guide. Make a sample and measure it for accuracy.

PIECING CURVES

Fold each curved piece in half to find the center of the seam. Clip the concave curve ³⁄₁₆ inch deep approximately every ½ inch along the curve (clip

more often for a very tight curve, less often for a gradual curve). With the two pieces' right sides together, match the center of each seam and the end points. Pin carefully. With the concave curve on top, stitch the pieces slowly, easing the fabric so that the edges stay even.

Chain Piecing for Efficiency

To streamline the sewing of multiple units, use chain piecing. Stitch a seam, and then without removing that unit from the sewing machine, insert the next unit to be stitched. Continue stitching from one unit to the

next. Make as many units as practical in one long chain. Then snip the threads connecting the units and press each unit. During the course of a project, this technique can save a substantial amount of time.

Strip Piecing

Strip piecing is another technique that can

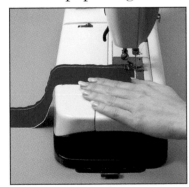

save lots of time when making quilts with complex blocks. Instead of using templates, cut strips of fabric. (Use a rotary cutter and a ruler for the greatest efficiency.) Stitch the strips of fabric together.

Then cut the strips and recombine the resulting units. See individual projects for specific instructions.

Hand Appliqué

Prepare pieces of fabric to be appliquéd by hand by tracing around the template on the right side of the fabric. Add a ³⁄₁₆-inch seam allowance as you cut out each piece. Fold under the seam allowance along the marked seam line. Baste around each piece to hold the seam allowances turned under, clipping curves where necessary.

Pin the first piece to be stitched to the background. Hand stitch it to the background with a blind stitch or, for a more decorative look, use a blanket stitch and contrasting thread.

When the appliqué is complete, consider carefully trimming the background fabric from behind the appliqué inside the stitching line. This must be done with great care so that the appliqué is not snipped, but it does reduce the bulk and make quilting easier.

MACHINE APPLIQUÉ

For machine appliqué, there is no seam allowance added to pattern pieces. Use fusible webbing to hold the appliqué firmly in place. Follow the manufacturer's instructions to iron fusible webbing to  the wrong side of the appliqué fabric. Trace the pattern piece on the paper side of the fusible webbing, cut out the appliqué, and follow the manufacturer's instructions to bond it to the background fabric. (For the quilts in this book, always place the pattern piece faceup on the paper side of the fusible webbing to trace the appliqué shape, unless otherwise instructed.) Stitch around the appliqué using a ⅛-inch- to ³⁄₁₆-inch-wide zigzag stitch. The stitches should be close together, but not so close that the fabric does not feed smoothly through the machine.

FINISHING TOUCHES

ASSEMBLING THE QUILT TOP

For a traditional quilt, arrange the completed quilt blocks. Sew the blocks together to form rows. Press. Sew the rows together. For quilts not made up of blocks, follow instructions for the individual projects to assemble.

PRESSING

Press completed quilt blocks from the back first and then lightly from the front. Do not apply pressure because this may stretch and distort the fabric. Instead, rely on lots of steam.

Press the completed quilt top before basting it to the batting and backing. Do not press a quilt once the batting has been added, because this will flatten it.

ADDING BORDERS

Add borders that are not quilt pieces simply by sewing strips of fabric (of the desired width) to the long sides of the quilt. Trim the ends of the strips even with the short sides of the quilt. Then  stitch strips of fabric to the short sides, stitching across the borders previously applied.

Press the borders and the seam allowances away from the center of the quilt. If there is more than one border, apply the borders in the same order for each.

In certain quilts, mitered corners, which require a little more time and care, look better than the square or butted corners above. Find the center of each border strip and the center of each side of the quilt. One side at a time, pin the border and stitch, beginning and ending ¼ inch from the edge of the quilt top. (Borders need strips longer than the sides for mitering.)

With right sides together, fold the quilt top diagonally, taking care to match seams and the edges of the borders. Use a ruler and pencil to extend across the border strips to the line formed by the fold.

Taking care not to snag seam allowances, stitch from the inside edge of the border to the outer corner on the marked line. Trim the ends of the border strips and press the seam open. Repeat for each corner.

FINISHING THE OUTER EDGES

Decide how you will finish the outer edges of your quilt before you prepare for quilting. Traditionally, the outer edges of quilts are encased in binding after the quilt is quilted. The binding wears better than other options, so the time spent applying the binding is worth it if you want the quilt to last a long time. Binding techniques are described on pages 19–20.

Some faster techniques, however, are done before the quilt is quilted. They include placing the right sides of the quilt top and backing together over the batting and stitching around the outside edges, leaving an opening through which the quilt is turned. Then the opening is slip-stitched closed.

PREPARATION FOR QUILTING

Decide what designs the quilting stitches will make. For a traditional look, outline important elements of the design with quilting. A grid of stitching works well in background areas. Fancier design elements that complement the theme of the quilt can also be incorporated. Make sure that there will be some stitching every few inches to secure the batting so that it does not shift.

Decide now if you need to mark the top for quilting. Simple outlining for grids can be marked with masking tape as you quilt. For more elaborate quilting designs, mark the top with one of the marking tools described on page 10. Use the lightest mark possible. Dark marks may be difficult to remove when the quilt is finished.

Spread out the backing (right side down) on a table or other flat surface. Use masking tape to secure the backing after smoothing it out. Place the batting on top of the backing, smoothing it out also. Finally, place the  completed quilt top on the backing, right side up. Stretch it out so it is smooth, and tape it.

For hand quilting, baste the layers together using long stitches. For best results, start basting at the center of the quilt and work toward the edges. Create a grid of basting by making a line of stitching roughly every four inches.

For machine quilting, baste by hand as described above or use safety pins. Place a safety pin every three or four inches. In order to save time later, avoid placing pins on quilting lines.

QUILTING

Quilting—stitching that goes through all three layers of the quilt—is both functional and decorative. It holds the batting in place. It is also an important design element, greatly enhancing the texture of the finished quilt. Hand quilting has a beautiful, classic appearance that cannot be duplicated, but it requires much more time than machine quilting. Machine quilting can be more dramatic because the tension of the stitches tends to create more extreme peaks and valleys. It is much faster and wears well.

To outline design areas, stitch ¼ inch away from each seam line. Simply decide where to stitch by eye or use ¼-inch masking tape placed along each seam as a guide. Masking tape can also be used as guides for straight lines and grids. Stitch beside the edge of the tape, avoiding stitching through the tape and getting adhesive on the needle and thread. Do not leave the masking tape on the fabric when you are finished stitching each day, however, because it can leave a sticky residue that is difficult to remove.

HAND QUILTING

Some quilters hold their work unsupported in their lap when they quilt. Most quilters, however, prefer to use some sort of quilting hoop or frame to hold the quilt stretched out. This makes it easier to stitch with an even tension and helps to prevent puckering and tucks.

Use betweens (quilting needles) for hand quilting. The smaller the needle (higher numbers like 11 and 12), the easier it will be to make small stitches. A quilting thimble on the third finger of your quilting hand will protect you from needle sores.

Use no more than 18 inches of quilting thread at a time. Longer pieces of thread tend to tangle, and the end gets worn as it is pulled through the fabric. Knot the end of the thread with a quilter's knot. Slip the needle into the quilt top and batting about an inch from where the first stitch should start. Pull the needle up through the quilt top at the beginning of the first stitch. Hold the thread firmly and give it a little tug. The knot should pop into the batting and lodge between the quilt top and backing.

The quilting stitch is a running stitch. Place your free hand (left hand for right-handed people) under the quilt to feel for the needle as it pokes through. Load the needle with a couple of stitches by rocking the needle  back and forth. At first, focus on making evenly sized stitches. Also, make sure you are going through all three layers. When you have mastered that, work on making the stitches smaller on future quilts.

MACHINE QUILTING

Machine quilting is easy to learn, but it does take some practice. Make a few trial runs before starting to stitch on your completed quilt. On the test swatch, adjust the tension settings for the machine so that the stitches are even and do not pucker or have loose loops of thread.

The easiest machine stitching is long straight lines, starting at the center of the quilt and radiating out. These lines may be in a grid, stitched in the ditches formed by seams, outlines around design elements, or channels (long, evenly spaced lines).

Whatever the pattern, quilt from the center to the outer edges. Plan the order of stitching. Your plan should minimize the need to start and stop as much as possible.

Before placing the quilt on the sewing machine, roll the sides in toward the center and secure the rolls with pins or bicycle clips. Use an even-feed walking foot for straight lines of stitching. For freehand stitching, use a darning foot and lower the feed dogs or use a throat plate that covers the feed dogs.

To begin, turn the handwheel to lower and raise the needle to its highest point. Pull gently on the top thread to bring the bobbin thread up through the quilt. Stitch in place for several stitches. Gradually increase the length of each stitch for the first ½ inch of quilting until the stitches are the desired length. This will secure the ends of the threads, making it unnecessary to backstitch or knot them. Reverse these steps at the end of each line of quilting.

When quilting with the even-feed walking foot, place your hands on either side of the presser foot and apply an even pressure. Keep the layers smooth and free of tucks.

When doing free-hand quilting, place your hands around the darning foot and apply gentle outward pressure to keep the layers smooth. Guide the fabric with smooth, even motions of the wrist. In freehand quilting, the fabric is free to move in any direction; it is not fed through the machine by the feed dogs. The stitch length is determined by the speed of the needle and the motion of the fabric under the needle. To keep the stitches the same length, maintain a steady speed and even motions. It takes some practice to get smooth curves and even stitch lengths using this technique, so don't be discouraged if your first attempts are a bit rough.

TYING QUILTS

The fastest way to secure the layers of a quilt (top, batting, and backing) together is to tie them. Thread a needle with a long piece of embroidery floss, yarn, or pearl cotton. At regular intervals (every four inches, at most) take a single stitch through the three layers of quilt. Tie the thread in a double square knot and trim the thread to a consistent length, usually ½ or 1 inch.

If you prefer, you can tie your quilt by machine. Baste as usual. Place the quilt on the machine and make sure all the layers are smooth. Set the stitch length and width at 0. Take several stitches and then increase the stitch width to a wide setting. Make about eight stitches and return the stitch width to 0. Make several stitches and clip the threads. Repeat until the quilt is tied at regular intervals.

To make the ties more decorative, make little bows from six-inch lengths of ribbon and stitch them in place, using the zigzag stitch as just described. Alternately, if your machine makes decorative stitches, use a decorative stitch instead of the zigazg stitch.

BINDING

Binding may be made from strips of fabric that match or coordinate with the fabrics used in the quilt. These strips may be cut on the straight grain or on the bias. Straight binding is easier to cut and apply and can be used on most of the projects in this book. Quilts that have curved edges require bias binding. Also, bias binding is stronger and tends to last longer. You can also purchase quilt binding and apply it according to the manufacturer's instructions.

To make straight binding, cut strips of fabric 3¼ inches wide (or follow directions for individual quilts) on the lengthwise or crosswise grain. For each side of the quilt you will need a strip the length of that side plus two inches. For example, if the side measures 40 inches long, cut your strips 42 inches long.

Baste around the quilt ¼ inch from the outer edge. Make sure all corners are square, and trim any excess batting or fabric. Prepare each strip of binding by folding it in half lengthwise, wrong sides together, and press. Find the center of each strip. Also find the center of each side of the quilt.

Place the binding strip on top of the quilt, aligning the raw edges of the strip and of the quilt and matching the centers. Stitch a ½-inch seam from one end of the quilt to the other. If you use an even-feed walking foot instead of the regular presser foot, it will be easier to keep the binding and the quilt smooth.

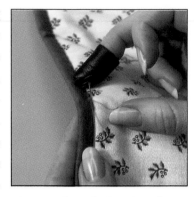

Trim excess binding from each end. Fold the binding to the back of the quilt, and slip-stitch it in place. Repeat for the opposite side of the quilt. Attach the binding to the other two sides of the quilt using the same procedure, but do not trim the ends of the binding. Instead, fold the excess binding over the end of the quilt. Holding the end in place, fold the binding to the back of the quilt and slip-stitch in place.

Making a Hanging Sleeve

To make a sleeve for hanging a quilt, cut a strip of fabric (muslin or a scrap of backing fabric) six inches wide and as long as the quilt is wide. To finish the ends of the strip, roll under the ends to the wrong side of the fabric and slip-stitch (or machine stitch). Fold the fabric lengthwise with wrong sides together. Stitch a ⅜-inch seam the length of the sleeve. Turn the sleeve wrong side out and press the seam. Stitch a ⅝-inch seam over the first seam. Turn the sleeve right side out and press. Stitch the sleeve to the top of the quilt and insert a dowel to hang the quilt.

MAKING A LABEL

All quilts should have a label with the quilter's name and date. Years after a quilt was made and its original purpose forgotten, it is exciting to discover that the maker documented the occasion with information such as why and for whom the quilt was made. Consider putting your thoughts and feelings on a label for each quilt.

Labels can be elaborate displays of needlework done in embroidery or counted cross-stitch, or they can be quick and simple. Use colored pens and calligraphy to get fancier. A leftover block makes a nice label. Write on it with a permanent pen and then appliqué it to the back of the quilt. The possibilities are endless.

In the space of a weekend, you can make a gift that sends a special message for a special someone. Pick out some beautiful fabrics and put them together in a wonderful new way. As time passes, your quilt is bound to become a family treasure, cherished by all who sense its warm message. Happy quilting!

WONDERFUL WALL QUILTS

Looking for an original way to liven up a room? Why not try a quilted wall hanging? A handmade quilt is a terrific, inexpensive way to personalize a room. And think how proud you'll feel when your guests ask you where you found your fabulous wall decorations!

In this chapter you'll find a variety of exciting wall hangings. If you're looking for a contemporary Southwest touch, try the easy-as-pie Navajo Rug. Watermelon Treat and Down-Home Veggies will bring a warm country accent to any room. For a refreshing breath of the outdoors, put Garden of Delights or Bird's Eye View in a sunny spot. Whichever project you choose to make, remember to add a label to the back for an extra-personal touch.

NAVAJO RUG

 Easy

WALL HANGING

24

What You'll Need

- ⅝ yard dark brown tone-on-tone
- ⅝ yard rust tone-on-tone
- ¾ yard honey print
- ½ yard cream print
- ¼ yard gold print
- ¼ yard red print
- 30×48-inch piece backing fabric
- 30×48-inch piece low-loft polyester batting
- 1½ yards ultra-hold fusible webbing
- 1 package ultra-hold fusible strip webbing, ¼-inch roll

The woven Navajo rug is a recognized symbol of fine Native American folk art. This easy, almost no-sew fabric version uses authentic Navajo motifs and colors to create a strong Southwest accent.

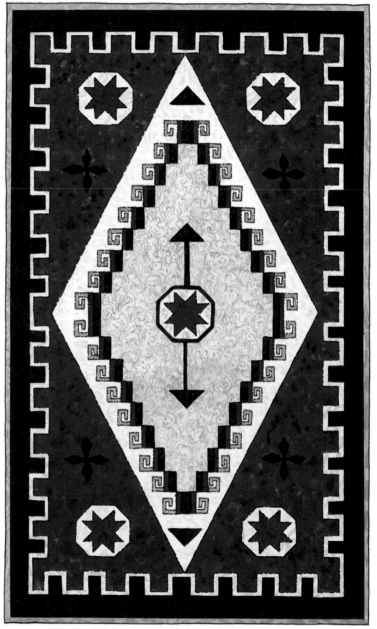

Dimensions: 27×46 inches

1. From dark brown, cut six 4×20-inch strips and four 4-inch squares on straight grain of fabric.

2. Trace and cut out all pattern pieces on page 29. Cut ¼ yard fusible webbing and iron to wrong side of remaining dark brown. Cut three ¾×18-inch strips. Remove paper backing. From strips, cut thirty-six ¾×1½-inch pieces. Trace and cut 1 octagonal C piece, 16 diamond-shaped D pieces, one 3½-inch square (cut diagonally in half twice to form 4 arrowheads), and two ¼×3¾-inch strips for arrow shafts. Remove all paper backing.

3. From each of rust, honey, and cream, cut two 10½×20½-inch rectangles. Cut each in half diagonally, forming 4 triangles.

4. Cut 9×17-inch piece fusible webbing and iron to wrong side of remaining rust. Cut thirty-two 1½-inch squares and six 1½×3-inch rectangles. Remove paper backing.

5. From remaining honey, cut six ½×27-inch binding strips. With right sides together, stitch 2 strips together to make ½×54-inch strip. Repeat to make another strip this size. Trim each long strip to 48 inches. Cut four 27-inch pieces and four 48-inch pieces from roll of fusible webbing and iron side by side to wrong side of fabric pieces. Remove paper backing.

6. Cut ½ yard fusible webbing and iron to wrong side of remaining cream. Trace and cut 5 octagonal B pieces. Cut seventeen ¼×17-inch strips. Remove paper backing. Cut six ¼×3¼-inch pieces. Cut rest of strips into ¼×1¾-inch pieces for a total of 150.

7. Cut ¼ yard fusible webbing and iron to wrong side of gold. Trace and cut out 18 E pieces. Turn over pattern piece and trace and cut out 18 reversed E pieces. Remove paper backing.

8. Cut ¼ yard fusible webbing and iron to wrong side of red. Trace and cut 5 piece A stars. Cut three ¼×18-inch strips. From these, cut thirty-six ¼×1½-inch strips. Remove paper backing.

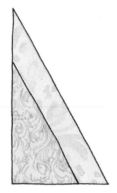

Step 9

9. On each honey triangle, draw a pencil line 2⅞ inches from edge of long side. Cut off edge along line. Iron a piece of fusible webbing from roll to wrong side of cut edge and remove paper backing. Place smaller honey triangle on top of cream triangle with right sides up. Align triangles with right-angle corners together and pin. Fuse long edge of honey triangle to cream triangle. Repeat for all 4 honey triangles.

Step 10

10. With right sides together, pin and stitch each honey/cream triangle to a rust triangle along long side, forming 4 rectangles. Press seams open. Join 2 rectangles along long sides to form an inner cream triangle, and repeat for other 2 rectangles. Join these 2 sections so honey/cream sections form an inner kite shape. Press all seams open.

11. With right sides together, stitch 2 brown border strips together to make a long 4×39½-inch strip. Repeat to make another long strip. Pin and stitch a long strip to each side of rust. Press seams to brown. Stitch brown square to each end of remaining 2 brown strips. Press seams to squares. Pin and stitch these strips to top and bottom of rust. Press seams toward top and bottom strips.

12. Center brown octagon and pin. Center cream octagon over it and red star on top. Fuse to honey background. For all fusing, refer to finished quilt illustration for placement.

13. Center 2 arrow shafts over vertical seams, touching but not overlapping brown octagon, and fuse. Place arrowhead at end of each shaft pointing out and fuse. Center remaining arrowheads on cream background in the same direction 6½ inches from brown edges and ½ inch from rust seams.

Step 14

14. Starting at top and bottom points of honey background, pin two ¾×1½-inch brown pieces side by side. Upper inside points should be on line between honey and cream, and bottom points should be on center seam and honey/cream line. Pin on remaining brown pieces with lower inner points and upper outer points on honey/cream line just touching each other. Brown pieces at center horizontal line will form ¾×3-inch rectangle. When all pieces are perfectly aligned, fuse.

15. Fuse a ¼×1½-inch red piece on top of each brown piece, exactly covering outer edge. Fuse gold figures into place.

16. Place cream octagon at each corner 5½ inches from side, top, and bottom edges. Fuse. Center and fuse red star on top of each octagon.

17. In each quadrant, place a pin 6¼ inches from side and 12 inches from top and bottom. This is center point of 4-pointed diamond stars. Place brown diamonds with points at pin. Fuse onto rust background.

18. Center and pin 1½×3-inch rust rectangle at midpoint of each side seam with long side on rust/brown seam. Place remaining rectangles at corners. Place 1½-inch squares spaced 1½ inches apart on seamline around entire brown border. When perfectly aligned, fuse.

Step 19

19. Center ¼×3¼-inch cream pieces over long edge of rust rectangles and fuse in place. Starting at a short side of one rectangle, center each ¼×1¾-inch cream piece over outer edge of a rust square and fuse. Center every fourth piece over rust/brown seam. Continue until design is complete.

20. Layer front, batting, and back and baste. Fold 27-inch honey binding strip in half lengthwise with wrong sides together. Encase top edge of quilt. Fuse binding to top edge, fusing first from front, then from back. Repeat for bottom edge. Repeat for sides, using 48-inch honey pieces. Trim ends even with top and bottom. If desired, layers may be yarn tied at regular intervals to provide additional stability.

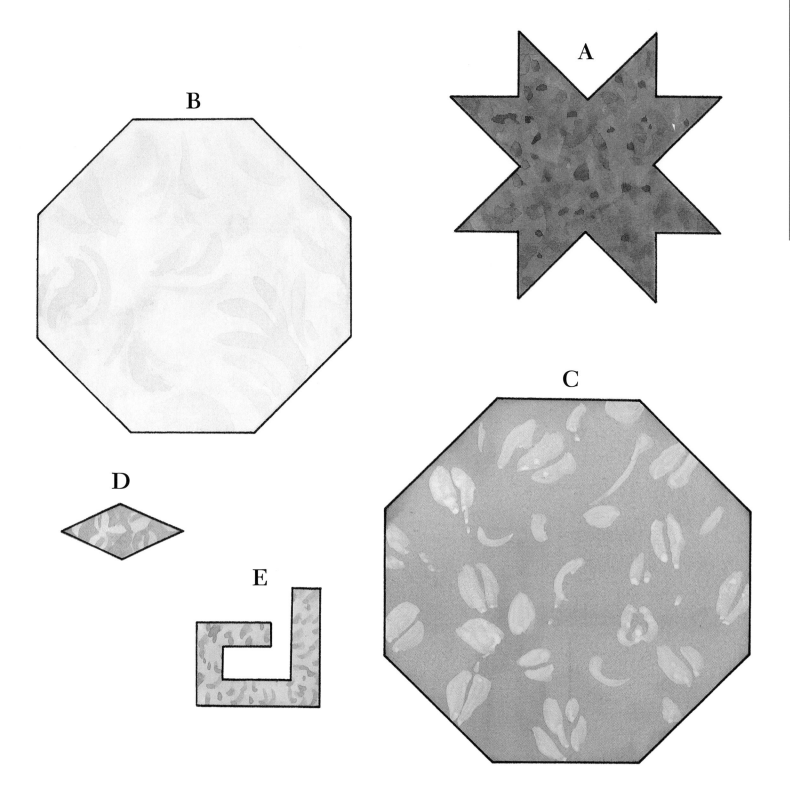

A

B

C

D

E

WATERMELON TREAT

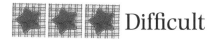 Difficult

WALL HANGING

What You'll Need

⅔ yard cream print

¼ yard black print for crow

½ yard black print for border

⅛ yard pink and black print

⅝ yard dark pink print

¼ yard green print

½ yard white print for border

⅛ yard white-on-white print

4-inch square yellow print

3-inch square dark brown print

½ yard backing fabric

40×18-inch piece low-loft batting

27 small black or dark brown buttons for watermelon seeds

1 round black button for crow's eye

White thread

Black thread

Conjure up memories of sunny summer days with this country quilt. Traditional piecing techniques and hand quilting create a feeling of old-fashioned charm.

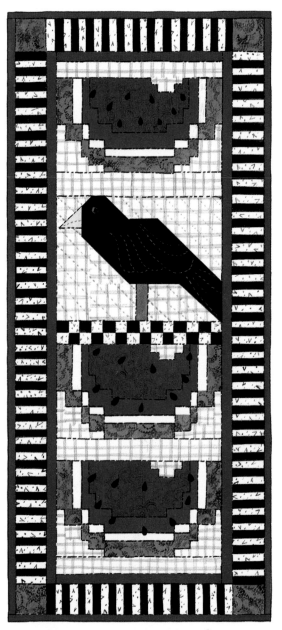

Dimensions: 16×38 inches

1. Start by assembling watermelon blocks. From cream print, cut one 1×12-inch strip, one 1×45-inch strip, and six 2× 2½-inch rectangles. From white-on-white, cut one 1×12-inch strip and one 1×45-inch strip. From pink and black print, cut two 1×45-inch strips and one 1½×45-inch strip. From dark pink, cut two 1×45-inch strips. From green, cut one 1½×45-inch strip, one 1½×12-inch strip, and one 1×45-inch strip. These quantities will make 3 watermelon blocks.

2. Stitch together one 1×45-inch dark pink strip, one 1×45-inch white-on-white strip, and one 1½×45-inch green strip lengthwise with white-on-white in middle. Press away from center.

3. Turn and cut sewn strip into three 5-inch lengths, six 3½-inch lengths, and six 1½-inch lengths. These will be A units.

4. Stitch together one 1×12-inch white-on-white strip, one 1½×12-inch green strip, and one 1×12-inch cream strip lengthwise with green in middle. Press toward center. Turn and cut sewn strip into six 1½-inch lengths. These will be B units.

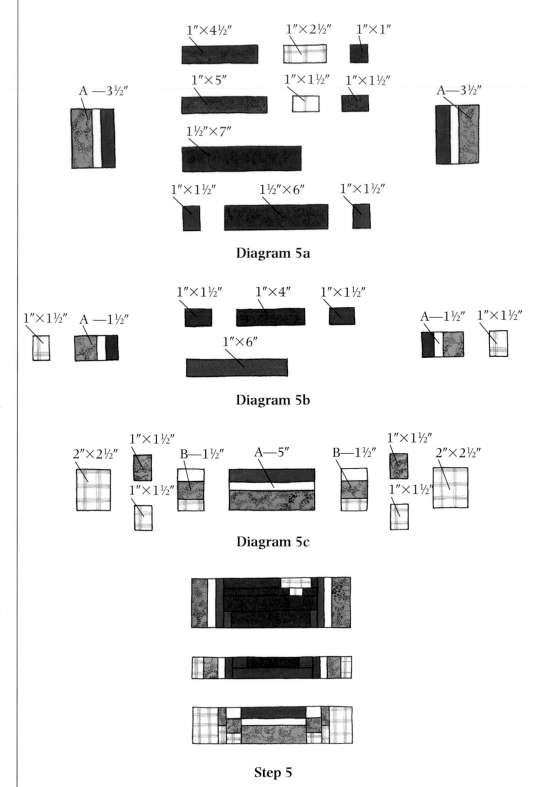

Diagram 5a

Diagram 5b

Diagram 5c

Step 5

32

5. From pink and black 1×45-inch strips, cut three 4½-inch lengths, three 1-inch lengths, three 5-inch lengths, three 1½-inch lengths, and three 4-inch lengths. From pink and black 1½×45-inch strip, cut three 7-inch lengths and three 6-inch lengths. From cream 1×45-inch strip, cut three 2½-inch lengths and fifteen 1½-inch lengths. From dark pink 1×45-inch strip, cut twelve 1½-inch lengths and three 6-inch lengths. From green 1×45-inch strip, cut six 1½-inch lengths. Follow diagrams to assemble strips, A units, and B units into 3 watermelon blocks. For each watermelon block, assemble pieces in diagram 5a, then pieces in diagram 5b, then pieces in diagram 5c. Finally, stitch all 3 sections together.

6. Assemble crow block in 4 sections. **Sections 1 and 2:** From cream, cut one 1×2-inch rectangle; one 1⅜-inch square, cut in half diagonally; one 2⅜-inch square, cut in half diagonally; one 2½×6½-inch rectangle; one 3-inch square; and one 3⅜-inch square, cut in half diagonally. From yellow, cut one 2⅜-inch square, cut in half diagonally. From black for crow, cut one 1⅜-inch square, cut in half diagonally; one 2⅜-inch square, cut in half diagonally; one 1×2-inch rectangle; one 1½×2-inch rectangle; one 2×3-inch rectangle; and one 3⅜-inch square, cut in half diagonally. **Section 3:** From cream, cut one 2×2½-inch rectangle, one 1×3-inch rectangle, and one 1¼×3-inch rectangle. From black for crow, cut one 2½×4½-inch rectangle. From dark brown, cut one 1¼×3-inch rectangle. **Section 4:** From cream, cut one 1½×3-inch rectangle; one 2×4½-inch rectangle; and one 4⅞-inch square, cut in half diagonally. From black for crow, cut one 1×3-inch rectangle and one 4⅞-inch square, cut in half diagonally. **Checkerboard:** From black for border, cut one 1¼×22-inch strip. From white for border, cut one 1¼×22-inch strip.

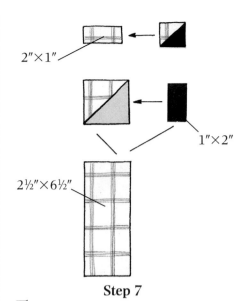

2"×1"

1"×2"

2½"×6½"

Step 7

7. Assemble section 1. With right sides together, stitch one 1⅜-inch cream triangle to one 1⅜-inch black triangle along diagonal sides. Press open. Do the same for one 2⅜-inch cream and one 2⅜-inch yellow triangle. Stitch section 1 together as shown in diagram.

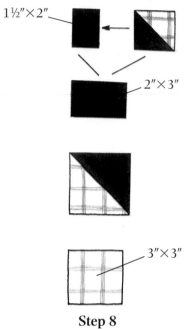

Step 8

8. Assemble section 2. With right sides together, stitch one 2⅜-inch black triangle to one 2⅜-inch cream triangle along diagonal sides. Press open. Do the same for one 3⅜-inch cream triangle and one 3⅜-inch black triangle. Stitch section 2 together as shown in diagram.

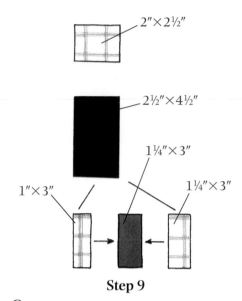

Step 9

9. Assemble section 3. Stitch pieces together as shown in diagram.

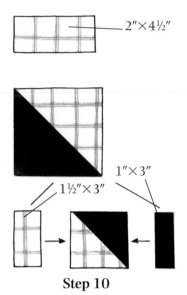

Step 10

10. Assemble section 4. With right sides together, stitch one 4⅞-inch black triangle to one 4⅞-inch cream triangle along diagonal sides. Press open. Do the same for one 3⅜-inch cream and one 3⅜-inch black triangle. The 3⅜-inch triangles come from sections 1 and 2 cutting (see Step 6). Stitch together section 4 as shown in diagram. Press each section in alternating directions (section 1 up, section 2 down, etc.). Stitch together sections 1, 2, 3, and 4 from left to right and press to one side. Finished crow block should measure 11×18 inches.

11. Assemble checkerboard. Stitch black and white strips together lengthwise. Press to dark. Turn and cut into fourteen 1¼-inch sections. Stitch sections together, alternating colors, to create checkerboard pattern.

12. Assemble sections and inner border. From cream, cut two 1½×11-inch strips and two 2×11-inch strips. From dark pink, cut two 1½×11-inch strips and two 1¼×34½-inch strips. Starting at the top, stitch one 1½×11-inch dark pink strip to one 1½×11-inch cream strip lengthwise. Stitch to top of melon block with dark pink at top. Stitch one 2×11-inch cream strip to bottom of melon block. Stitch crow block to bottom of melon block plus strip. Stitch checkerboard strip to bottom of crow block. Stitch another melon block to bottom of checkerboard block. Stitch 2×11-inch cream strip to bottom of melon block. Stitch last melon block to bottom of melon block plus strip. Stitch 1½×11-inch cream strip to bottom of melon block. Stitch 1½×11-inch dark pink strip to bottom of melon block plus strip. Stitch long dark pink strips to sides of quilt. See finished quilt illustration.

13. Assemble piano key border. Cut six 1×45-inch strips from white for border and six 1×45-inch strips from black for border. For corner squares, cut four 2½-inch squares from green. Stitch all black and white strips together lengthwise, alternating colors. Press strips to dark as you stitch them together. Turn and cut into 2½-inch sections. Stitch sections together end to end, alternating colors. Count off 2 sections of 24 piano keys and stitch to top and bottom of quilt. Strip at top should have white key at left end. Strip at bottom should have black key at left end. Count off 2 sections of 68 piano keys. Stitch corner squares to each end and stitch to sides of quilt. Strip on left should have black key at top. Strip on right should have white key at top. Stay-stitch ⅛ inch away from edge of piano key border to prevent stretching while quilting.

14. Layer front, batting, and back and baste. With white thread, hand quilt in ditches between borders and blocks. Hand quilt lines on edges of black keys in piano key border and lines in melons, backgrounds, and crow. Hand quilt hearts in green corner squares. With black thread, hand quilt diagonal lines in crow block and crow's beak. To save time or create a different look, machine quilt your designs. Use black thread to stitch round button to crow face and remaining buttons to melons for watermelon seeds. Our buttons were hand-made from polymer clay. You may also purchase small buttons to make watermelon seeds. From binding fabric, cut three 3¼×45-inch strips. Follow directions on pages 19–20 to stitch binding to quilt.

BIRD'S EYE VIEW

 Easy

WALL HANGING

36

What You'll Need

¼ yard medium blue

¼ yard light blue

⅛ yard light green

⅛ yard pig print

⅛ yard gold flower print

⅛ yard cow print

⅛ yard sunflower print

¼ yard dark green flower print

⅛ yard dark brown and black plaid

¼ yard dark green print

⅜ yard dark red plaid

¼ yard black

⅛ yard each or scraps white, red, blue, and straw-colored prints

⅞ yard backing fabric

29×38-inch piece batting

⅛ yard or scraps lightweight fusible webbing

Fabric stabilizer

Medium gray thread

Transparent monofilament thread

Black fine-point marker

Bring the outdoors in with this easy-as-pie wall hanging! Select dark, large-print fabrics for the foreground, progressing to very light fabrics at the horizon to create a sense of perspective.

Dimensions: 25×34 inches

1. Trace and cut out scarecrow patterns on page 39. Iron fusible webbing to wrong side of white, red, blue, and straw-colored prints. Trace scarecrow patterns onto paper side of fusible webbing and cut out. Remove paper backing and set aside scarecrow pieces.

2. From medium blue, cut one 7½×19½-inch rectangle. From light blue, cut one 6×19½-inch rectangle. From light green, cut one 1½×19½-inch strip. From pig fabric, cut one 2×19½-inch strip. From gold flower print, cut one 2½×19½-inch strip. From cow print, cut one 2½×19½-inch strip. From sunflower print, cut one 2½×19½-inch strip. From dark green flower print, cut one 4½×19½-inch strip. From black and brown plaid, cut one 3½×19½-inch strip. From dark green, cut two 1½×32½-inch strips and two 1½×23½-inch strips. From dark red plaid, cut two 2½×36½-inch strips and two 2½×27½-inch strips. From black, cut three 2×44-inch strips. From backing fabric, cut one 31×40-inch piece.

3. Arrange all fabrics representing fields and sky in desired order (see finished quilt illustration for placement). Do not include black and brown plaid piece. Stitch field and sky pieces together.

4. Arrange scarecrow pieces on lower left corner of dark green flower print strip. Left arm and lower edge of jacket should extend into lower seam allowance. Fuse pieces in the following order: hand, jacket, face, handkerchief, brim of hat, top of hat. Cut piece of stabilizer larger than scarecrow and pin to wrong side of quilt top under scarecrow. With transparent thread and narrow zigzag stitch, machine stitch around each appliqué piece. Remove fabric stabilizer. Use black marker to outline hat, draw hat brim, and add detail to hand.

5. Stitch black and brown plaid piece to lower edge of quilt top, including lower edge of appliqué in seam. Press.

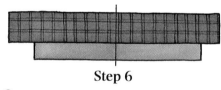

Step 6

6. To make side borders, fold dark green 1½×32½-inch border strip in half lengthwise and mark center. Repeat for red plaid 2½×36½-inch border strip. With centers matching, stitch strips together lengthwise. Ends of strips will not line up. Repeat for other red plaid and dark green strip of same length.

7. Find center of each dark green 1½×23½-inch strip and each 2½×27½-inch red plaid strip. Match centers and stitch each 1½×23½-inch strip to a 2½×27½-inch strip to make the top and bottom borders.

8. Find and mark center of each edge of quilt top. With centers matched, stitch borders to edges of quilt top. Follow directions on page 15 to miter corners.

9. Layer quilt front, batting, and back and baste. Using transparent thread, quilt in ditches around borders. Quilt straight horizontal lines in black and brown plaid. Quilt diagonal lines radiating outward from scarecrow. Follow directions on page 15 to stitch black binding to quilt.

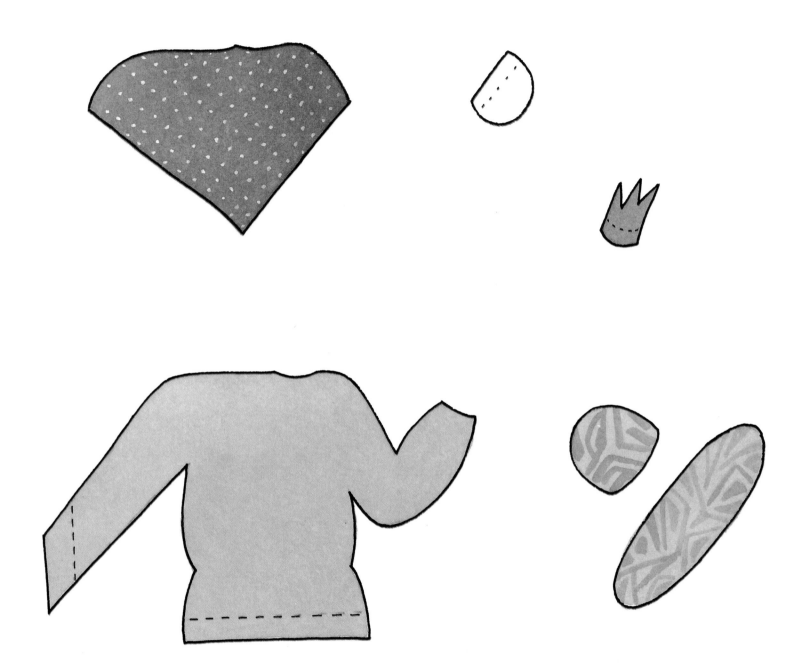

39

GARDEN OF DELIGHTS

 Easy

WALL HANGING

What You'll Need

¼ yard green flower print

¼ yard light green print

¼ yard light yellow print

¼ yard medium to light blue print

¼ yard light blue print

¼ yard light tan print

⅛ yard brown print

¼ yard light brown print

22×27-inch piece backing fabric

¼ yard solid dark brown

22×27-inch piece cotton batting

1 yard fusible webbing

½-inch bias tape maker

4 black beads, 4mm

2 yellow buttons, ⅝-inch

Black, dark green, red, and white rayon machine embroidery threads

Rayon machine embroidery threads to match appliqués

1×8-inch strip solid brown

15½-inch square olive green print for stems

15½-inch square dark green print for stems

Appliqué fabrics:

6-inch squares: 1 each of bright yellow print, bright pink print, bright red print, dark red print, tan and black check, and medium green print

4-inch squares: 1 each of dark purple print, light purple print, bright blue print

continued on page 42

Spring has sprung in this delightful scene.
Simple appliqué techniques will help
you quickly make this colorful wall hanging
and enjoy a hint of warm sunshine
in any season.

Dimensions: 21½×26½ inches

Appliqué fabrics, continued:

5-inch squares: 1 each of brown check and dark brown print

2½-inch squares: 1 each of medium purple print, bright blue print, and black

8-inch square dark green print

Hint: Instead of making your own bias tape in step 3, you may also purchase premade bias tape.

1. Trace and cut out all patterns on pages 44–46. Iron fusible webbing to wrong side of all appliqué fabrics. Trace all appliqué shapes on paper side of fusible webbing. Refer to finished quilt illustration to match shapes to fabric squares.

2. From green flower print, cut two 5½-inch squares. From light green print, cut one 5½-inch square. From light yellow print, cut one 5½-inch square. From medium to light blue print, cut one 5½-inch square and one 5½×15½-inch rectangle. From light blue print, cut one 5½×10½-inch rectangle. From light tan print, cut one 5½×10½-inch square.

3. From 15½-inch olive green square, cut four 1-inch-wide strips on the bias. If you are using a bias tape maker, follow manufacturer's instructions to fold and press each long side ¼ inch to wrong side to make ½-inch bias strip. If not using a tape maker, use iron to fold and press each long side ¼ inch to wrong side. Fold and press 2 of the strips in half to make ¼-inch bias tape. From 15½-inch dark green square, cut two 1-inch-wide strips. As with olive strips, make ¼-inch bias tape from both strips.

4. Make block 1. Trace and cut out sunflower, sunflower center, and 3 leaves. Cut olive green ½-inch bias strip 5½ inches long. Following illustration, pin ½-inch bias strip to light blue 5½×10½-inch rectangle for stem. Cut three 1¼-inch lengths from olive green ¼-inch bias and pin to blue background, tucking ends under ½-inch-wide stem. Stitch stem pieces to blue background with straight stitch along edges, using dark green or black rayon machine embroidery thread. Fuse sunflower and leaves to light blue background, covering raw edges of bias stems. Fuse sunflower center to sunflower. Using blanket stitch and matching rayon machine embroidery threads, stitch around flower, center, and leaves.

5. Make blocks 2, 4, and 8. Refer to illustration for placement. For block 2, trace and cut out 2 flowers, 2 flower centers, and 3 leaves. Fuse flowers, centers, and leaves to 5½-inch light green square. For block 4, trace and cut out 2 butterflies. Fuse butterflies to 5½-inch light yellow square. For block 8, trace and cut out 8 ladybugs. Fuse ladybugs to 5½-inch green flower square. Blanket stitch around edges of flowers, flower centers, leaves, and butterflies with matching machine embroidery threads. Do not stitch around ladybugs.

6. Make block 5. Trace and cut out 2 cardinals, 2 beaks, and 2 leaves. Fuse cardinals to 5½-inch green flower print square. Blanket stitch around edges with red rayon machine embroidery thread. Fuse cardinal beaks to cardinal shapes. Cut 6-inch strip from dark green ¼-inch bias and pin beneath cardinals. Stitch to background with straight stitch along edges, using dark green or black rayon machine embroidery thread. Fuse leaves and blanket stitch around edges with green rayon machine embroidery thread.

7. Make block 3. Trace and cut out 2 flowers, 2 flower centers, and 3 leaves. From dark green ¼-inch bias tape, cut two 1-inch pieces, one 3¼-inch piece, and one 4¼-inch piece. Following illustration, pin ¼-inch bias stems in place on 5½-inch medium to light blue square. Stitch to background with straight stitch along edges, using dark green or black rayon machine embroidery thread. Fuse flowers and leaves to background, covering raw edges of stems. Fuse flower centers to flowers. Blanket stitch around flower and leaf edges, using matching rayon machine embroidery thread.

8. Make block 7. Trace and cut out all parts of birdhouse, post, bird, and 6 leaves. Fuse birdhouse pieces, post, and bird to 5½×15½-inch medium to light blue rectangle. Blanket stitch around edges of birdhouse and bird with matching rayon machine embroidery thread. Cut one 15-inch piece from olive green ¼-inch bias tape. Pin in place as vine stem. Stitch to blue background with straight stitch along edges, using dark green or black rayon machine embroidery thread. Fuse leaves and blanket stitch around edges, using slightly contrasting rayon machine embroidery thread.

9. Make block 6. Trace and cut out 2 flowers, 2 flower centers, 2 large leaves, and 1 small leaf. From olive green ½-inch bias tape, cut one 4¼-inch piece and one 6¼-inch piece. Pin stems in place on 5½×10½-inch light tan piece. Fuse leaves to tan background, tucking bottom edges under stems. Blanket stitch around edges, using dark green or black rayon machine embroidery thread. Stitch stems in place with straight stitch along edges, using dark green or black rayon machine embroidery thread. Do not fuse flowers to background yet.

10. Referring to finished quilt illustration, stitch all blocks together.

11. Fuse flowers and centers in block 6, covering raw edges of stems. Flower on left should overlap seam. Blanket stitch around edges with matching rayon machine embroidery thread.

12. Cut two 1×45-inch strips from brown print for inner border. Measure quilt vertically through center and cut 1 strip this length from each 45-inch strip. Stitch to sides of quilt. Measure quilt horizontally through center and cut remaining strips to this length. Stitch to top and bottom of quilt. Press.

13. Cut three 2½×45-inch strips from light brown print for outer border. Stitch 1 strip to each side. Cut remaining strip in half and stitch to top and bottom. Press.

14. Layer quilt front, batting, and back and baste. With white thread, machine quilt in ditches between blocks and around borders and outline quilt around shapes. Use black thread to quilt around ladybugs and to quilt lines defining ladybug wings and heads. Sew beads to cardinal faces for eyes. Sew yellow buttons to block 3 flower centers.

15. Cut three 2½×45-inch dark brown strips for binding. Follow directions on pages 19–20 to stitch binding to quilt.

Block 2 flower center

Block 2 leaf

Block 2 flower

Block 5 leaf

Block 6 flower

Block 7 birdhouse

44

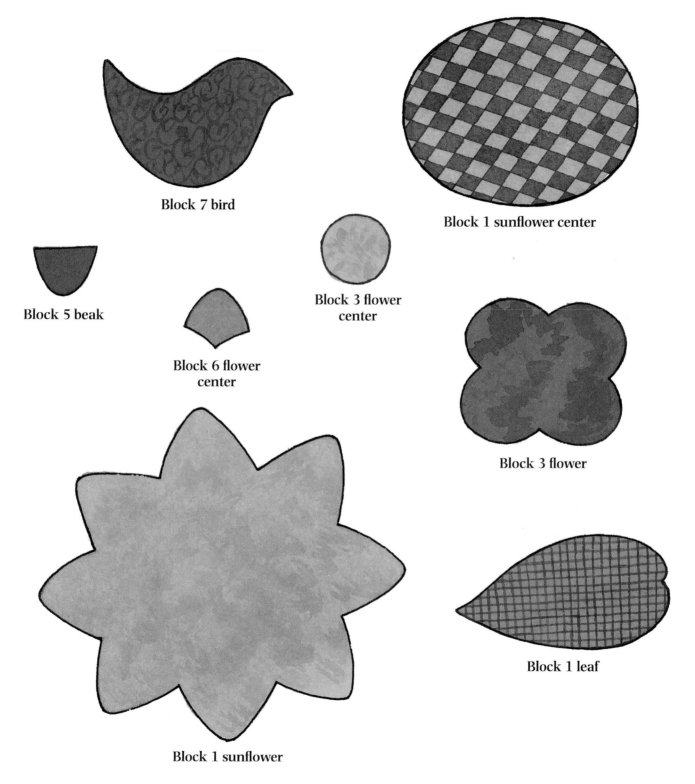

Block 7 bird

Block 1 sunflower center

Block 5 beak

Block 3 flower
center

Block 6 flower
center

Block 3 flower

Block 1 sunflower

Block 1 leaf

45

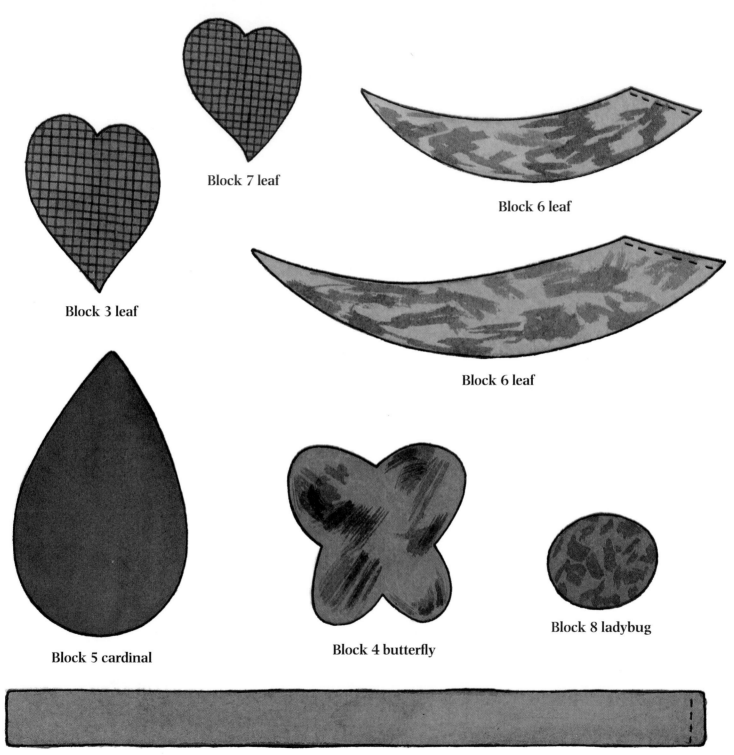

Block 7 leaf

Block 6 leaf

Block 3 leaf

Block 6 leaf

Block 5 cardinal

Block 4 butterfly

Block 8 ladybug

Block 7 post

Down-Home Veggies

 Moderate

WALL HANGINGS

What You'll Need

For each quilt:

⅛ yard each or scraps 8 different fabrics for borders; colors should harmonize with central block

9×12-inch piece backing fabric

¼ yard binding fabric

9×12-inch piece low-loft batting

8 buttons in assorted colors and sizes

Jute for tying on buttons

White thread for hand quilting

For Eggplant:

⅛ yard cream print

⅛ yard purple print

⅛ yard dark green print

Dark green thread

For Onion:

⅛ yard cream print

⅛ yard yellow print

⅛ yard medium green print

40-inch length jute

For Carrot:

⅛ yard tan print

⅛ yard orange print

⅛ yard green and cream print

For Radish:

⅛ yard tan print

⅛ yard red print

⅛ yard dark green print

⅛ yard or scrap white-on-white print

2½-inch length jute

Dark green thread

Give your kitchen a warm country touch with these appetizing wall hangings! Each quilt can be made entirely with fabric scraps and buttons from your sewing basket.

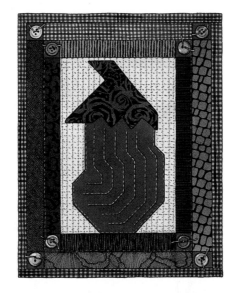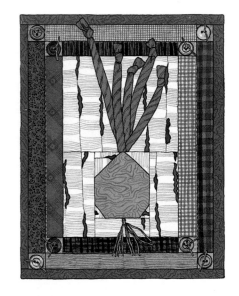

Dimensions: 8½×11 inches each

48

For these quilts, you will use the bias rectangle and template-free angle piecing techniques.

TEMPLATE-FREE ANGLE PIECING

TO ADD A SQUARE:

Draw a diagonal line from corner to corner on wrong side of fabric square. Following diagram, lay square on other fabric piece with right sides together. Stitch on diagonal line and cut away ¼ inch from seam, on outer side. Press open. To add a second square, repeat steps, but with diagonal line going in opposite direction.

TO ADD A LARGER PIECE:

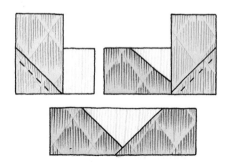

Lay fabric pieces with right sides together as shown in diagram. Draw diagonal line from corner

to corner of square formed where top fabric covers bottom fabric. Stitch on line, cut away ¼ inch from seam, and press open. To add a second piece, repeat steps as shown in diagram.

BIAS RECTANGLES

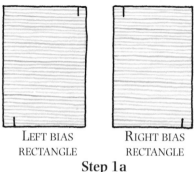

LEFT BIAS RECTANGLE   RIGHT BIAS RECTANGLE

Step 1a

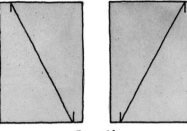

Step 1b

1. Cut equal-size rectangles of background fabric and contrast fabric. On right side of background fabric, mark ⅛ inch in from outside edges at top and bottom. On wrong side of contrast fabric, mark ⅛ inch in from outside edges at top and bottom. Note that the marks are opposite for right and left bias rectangles. On wrong side of contrast pieces only, draw diagonal line linking the ⅛-inch marks.

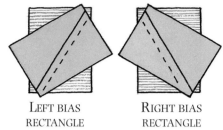

LEFT BIAS RECTANGLE   RIGHT BIAS RECTANGLE

Step 2

2. With right sides together, place contrast fabric on top of background fabric. For a right bias rectangle, turn contrast rectangle counterclockwise until upper right corner is within ⅛ inch of upper left corner of background rectangle and lower left corner is within ⅛ inch of lower right corner of background. For a left bias rectangle, turn contrast rectangle clockwise until upper left corner is within ⅛ inch of upper right corner of background and lower right corner is within ⅛ inch of lower left corner of background.

3. Stitch on line. Cut away excess, leaving ¼-inch seam allowance. (See dotted lines in step 2 diagram.) Open and press. If making more than one bias rectangle, use chain piecing technique described on page 13.

GENERAL DIRECTIONS FOR BORDERS

Follow these general directions to make borders for Down-Home Veggies quilts. Each border strip is cut from a different fabric. All corner squares for one quilt are the same color.

1. Cut two 1¼×8-inch strips (inner sides); two 1¼×5 ½-inch strips (inner top and bottom); two 1¼×9½-inch strips (outer sides); two 1¼×7-inch strips (outer top and bottom); and eight 1¼-inch squares. For binding cut one 2½×44-inch strip. Cut this strip into two 2½×11-inch strips for sides and two 2½×9½-inch strips for top and bottom.

2. Stitch one corner square to each end of top and bottom strips (1¼×5½ inches and 1¼×7 inches).

3. To finished vegetable block, stitch 1¼×8-inch side strips, then 1¼×5½-inch top and bottom strips (with corner squares). Add 1¼×9½-inch outer side strips, then 1¼×7-inch outer top and bottom strips with corner squares.

4. Sew buttons on each corner square with jute. Knot jute on top side.

5. Quilt as desired. Our quilts are hand quilted. To save time or create a slightly different look, you can machine quilt designs.

6. Follow directions on pages 19–20 to stitch binding to quilt.

DIRECTIONS FOR LEAVES AND TOPS

1. For each leaf or top, trace pattern piece on page 55 and cut out. Trace pattern on wrong side of fabric and cut out. Turn pattern over, trace, and cut out reversed shape. Each pattern has a line showing where to cut a slit for turning. Cut a slit in one piece only.

2. With right sides together, stitch matching leaf and top pieces together. Use ⅛-inch seam allowance and smaller stitches. When sewing points, it's easier to turn and get a smooth point if you stitch 1 stitch across the point. Trim all points and clip into corners.

3. Turn through slit opening on back (it's not necessary to close opening, since it will be on back side). Press. If desired, use white thread to hand stitch lines to represent leaf veins.

4. With slit to back, hand stitch tops and leaves to vegetable blocks, using dark green thread.

EGGPLANT

1. From cream print, cut one 1¾×18-inch strip and one 5½×2¾-inch rectangle. Cut strip into: two 1¾-inch squares, one 1½×3-inch rectangle, one 1½×2-inch rectangle, two 1×3¼-inch rectangles, one 1×1½-inch rectangle, and two 1-inch squares. From purple, cut one 3½×18-inch strip. Cut strip into: one 3½×2-inch piece, one 3¼×4½-inch piece, and one 1½×4-inch piece.

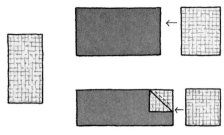

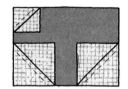

Step 2

2. Stitch 3½×2-inch purple piece to 1½×2-inch cream piece along 2-inch sides. Using template-free angle piecing, stitch 1-inch cream square to upper right corner of 4×1½-inch purple piece. Add 1×1½-inch cream piece to right side. Join units and add 1½×3-inch cream piece to left side.

Step 3

3. Using template-free angle piecing technique, stitch 1¾-inch cream squares to bottom corners of 4½×3¼-inch purple piece. Stitch 1-inch cream square to upper left corner of purple piece. Add one 1×3¼-inch cream piece to each side.

4. Assemble eggplant, adding 5½×2¾-inch cream piece to top.

5. Add border, following General Directions for Borders. Make eggplant top from dark green print, following Directions for Leaves and Tops.

6. Layer front, batting, and back and baste. With white thread, hand quilt in ditches around center block and between inner and outer borders. Hand quilt lines in eggplant and diagonal grid pattern in background. Follow directions on pages 19–20 to stitch binding to quilt.

ONION

1. From cream, cut one 4½×44-inch strip. Cut strip into: one 4½×5½-inch rectangle, one 4×2-inch rectangle, one 4×1¾-inch rectangle, one 2¾×1¼-inch rectangle, two 1½-inch squares, and two 1-inch squares. From yellow, cut one 2¾×3¼-inch rectangle. From green, cut one 1¼×44-inch strip.

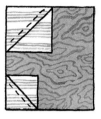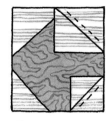

Step 2

2. Lay yellow rectangle right side up with short sides at top and bottom. Using template-free angle piecing technique, stitch 1½-inch cream square to upper left corner of yellow and 1-inch cream square to lower left corner. Open and press. Repeat for right side of yellow rectangle.

3. Fold green strip in half lengthwise with wrong side out and stitch. Turn. Cut into one 6½-inch strip, two 5½-inch strips, one 5-inch strip, and one 4½-inch strip. Tie a knot at 1 end of each strip.

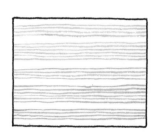

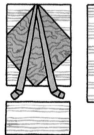

Step 4

4. Lay 2 green strips on top of onion unit with knotted ends out and unknotted ends at upper corner of onion. Stitch 4½×5½-inch cream piece to top of onion unit, including unknotted ends of green strips in seam. Stitch 2¾×1¼-inch cream piece to bottom of yellow. Stitch 4×2-inch cream piece to left side of yellow and 4×1¾-inch cream piece to right side of yellow.

5. Hand stitch remaining onion tops to quilt with unknotted ends behind two tops already sewn in. Fold all sewn tops up and stitch over ends of tops just added. Do not stitch knotted ends to background yet.

6. Add borders, following General Directions for Borders. Layer front, batting, and back and baste. With white thread, hand quilt in ditches around center block and between inner and outer borders. Hand quilt lines in onion. Follow directions on pages 19–20 to stitch binding to quilt.

7. Hand stitch knotted ends of onion to quilt. Cut eight 5-inch lengths of jute and tie a knot in center of lengths. Hand stitch knot to bottom of onion, allowing ends to hang down to form roots. Trim ends.

CARROT

1. From tan print, cut one 1¾×44-inch strip and one 5½×2¼-inch rectangle. Cut strip into: two 1¾×1½-inch rectangles, four 1¾×4¾-inch strips, two 1-inch squares, and one 1×5½-inch strip. From orange, cut one 1¾×22-inch strip. Cut strip into: two 1¾×4¾-inch pieces and one 3×1½-inch piece. From green and cream, cut one ¾×44-inch strip.

2. Using template-free angle piecing technique, stitch two 1-inch tan squares to upper corners of 3×1½-inch orange piece. Stitch one 1¾×1½-inch tan piece to each side of unit.

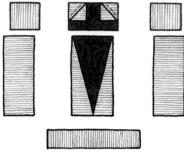

Step 3

3. Make 1 right and 1 left bias rectangle using 1¾×4¾-inch tan and orange pieces. Stitch together with orange on the inside, and add one 1¾×4¾-inch tan piece to each side of unit. Stitch 5½×1-inch tan strip to bottom. Stitch upper and lower parts of carrot together.

4. For carrot top, cut green strip into 4-, 5-, and 6-inch lengths. Fray edges. Gather random lengths together with ends even and twist ends together. You don't have to use all carrot top pieces.

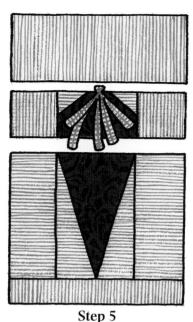

Step 5

5. Lay twisted ends of carrot tops at top of carrot unit in center of carrot. Stitch 5½×2¼-inch tan piece to top of carrot, including carrot top in seam. Flip up carrot top pieces and hand stitch to quilt about 1 inch above orange. Carrot top will extend over borders.

6. Add borders, following General Directions for Borders. Layer quilt front, batting, and back and baste. With white thread, hand quilt in ditches around center block and between inner and outer borders. Hand quilt curved lines in carrot and grid pattern in background. Follow directions on pages 19–20 to stitch binding to quilt.

RADISH

1. From tan print, cut one 3½×44-inch strip. Cut strip into: two 3½×1¼-inch strips, one 3×5½-inch rectangle, two 3×1¾-inch rectangles, two 1¾-inch squares, one 1¼×5½-inch strip, and two 1-inch squares. From red, cut one 4×3½-inch rectangle. From white, cut one 3×1¾-inch rectangle. From green, cut pieces to make 2 small leaves and 1 large leaf, following Directions for Leaves and Tops.

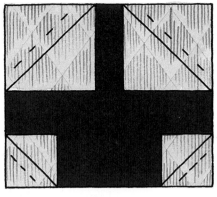

Step 2

2. Using template-free angle piecing, stitch two 1¾-inch tan squares to upper corners of red and two 1-inch tan squares to lower corners of red. Add one 1¼×3½-inch tan piece to each side of unit.

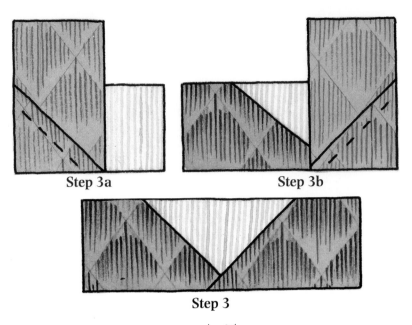

Step 3a   Step 3b

Step 3

3. Using template-free angle piecing technique, stitch 3×1¾-inch tan pieces to white. Stitch radish unit to root unit. Press. Stitch 5½×3-inch tan piece to top of radish.

4. For root, cut 2½-inch length of jute and tie knot in one end. Lay jute over root unit with unknotted end at point of root. Stitch 5½×1¼-inch tan piece to bottom of root unit, including unknotted end of jute in seam.

5. Make leaves, following Directions for Leaves and Tops. Using dark green thread, hand stitch to top of radish, as shown in photo.

6. Add borders, following General Directions for Borders. Layer front, batting, and back and baste. With white thread, hand quilt in ditches around center block and between inner and outer borders. Hand quilt curved lines in radish. Follow directions on pages 19–20 to stitch binding to quilt.

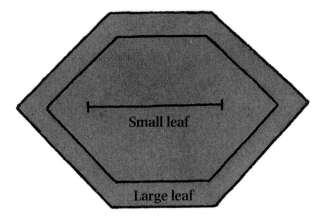

Small leaf

Large leaf

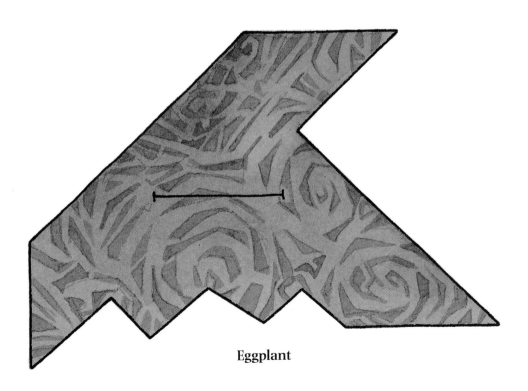

Eggplant

Fabulous Home
Decorations & Gifts

Everyone loves receiving lovingly handmade gifts. The quilts in this chapter are all delightful decorations for the home that you can keep or give away.

For the well-appointed kitchen, the Strawberry Fields breakfast set or Colonial House tea set are the perfect addition. For the dining room, you can set an elegant tone with the Casual Sophistication table set. The Daisy Chain and Stars & Stripes Forever lap quilts will add a cozy touch to any room, while the classic Vase of Lilies bed quilt brings a rich, Victorian note to your bedroom. And the Keepsake pillow will let you display cherished pieces of old lace. Be careful: By the time you've finished making one of these quilts as a gift, you may not be willing to part with it!

DAISY CHAIN

 Moderate

L A P   Q U I L T

58

What You'll Need

2 yards light blue flower print

1½ yards yellow flower print

½ yard yellow print

¼ yard medium blue flower print

⅛ yard brown print

½ yard green print

1 yard white-on-white print

2 yards backing fabric

1½ yards fusible webbing

50×65-inch piece low-loft batting

17 squares tissue paper, 8×8 inches

Yellow, green, and brown machine sewing threads to match appliqué fabrics

Light gray, white, and blue machine sewing threads

This cheery lap quilt is a contemporary version of the traditional nine-patch. It's perfect for snuggling up on a cool spring evening or for bringing sunny charm to any room all year round.

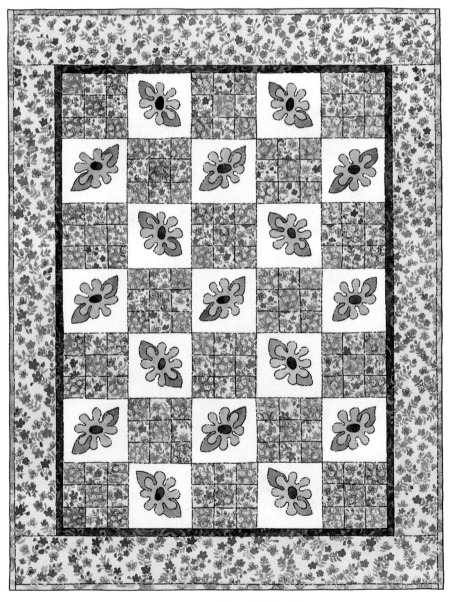

Dimensions: 45×60 inches

59

A strip set

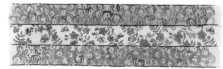

B strip set

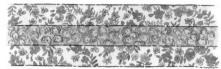

Step 1

1. From light blue print, cut eight 3×45-inch strips. From yellow flower print, cut seven 3×45-inch strips. Stitch 1 blue strip to each long side of 3 yellow strips. This makes 3 A strip sets. Stitch 1 yellow strip to each long side of 2 blue strips. This makes 2 B strip sets.

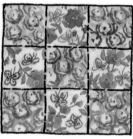

Step 2

2. Cut A strip sets into thirty-six 3-inch units. Cut B strip sets into eighteen 3-inch units. Keep A units separate from B units. Stitch 1 A unit to each side of 1 B unit, alternating colors to form a 9-patch. Make eighteen 9-patch squares.

3. From white-on-white, cut seventeen 8-inch squares. Trace and cut out all pattern pieces on page 61. Iron fusible webbing to wrong side of yellow, green, and brown prints. Trace daisy pattern 17 times on paper side of fusible webbing on yellow print. Trace each leaf pattern 17 times on paper side of fusible webbing on green print. Trace center 17 times on paper side of fusible webbing on brown print. Cut out all pieces and remove paper backing.

4. Referring to finished quilt illustration for placement, fuse 1 daisy, 1 center, and 2 leaves onto each white-on-white square.

5. Pin square of tissue paper to back of each daisy square. Thread machine with coordinating color thread and light gray thread in bobbin. Using zigzag stitch (2.5W-.5L), stitch around flowers, centers, and leaves. Tear off tissue paper.

6. Stitch blocks together, following finished quilt illustration.

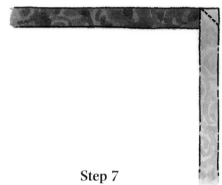

Step 7

7. From medium blue flower print, cut five 1½×45-inch strips. With right sides together, lay end of 1 strip over end of another strip at right angles. Draw a diagonal line from corner to corner of square formed where strips overlap. Stitch along line and cut away excess. Open and press. Repeat for other strips to form 1 continuous strip. Measure quilt vertically through center and cut 2 strips to that length from long strip. Stitch strips to sides of quilt and press. Measure quilt horizontally through center and cut 2 strips to that length from long strip. Stitch to top and bottom and press.

60

8. From yellow flower print, cut five 3½×45-inch strips. Stitch together to form one continuous strip, as in step 7. Measure quilt vertically through center and cut 2 strips to this length from long strip. Stitch to sides of quilt and press. Measure quilt horizontally through center and cut 2 strips to this length from long strip. Stitch to top and bottom and press.

9. Layer quilt front, batting, and backing and baste. With white thread, quilt in ditches around border and blocks. With blue thread, quilt "X" patterns through 9-patch blocks.

10. From light blue flower print, cut five 2½×45-inch strips. Follow directions on pages 19–20 to stitch binding to quilt.

KEEPSAKE

 Easy

PILLOW

62

What You'll Need

- 1 yard rose medium-weight fabric such as silk, moiré, or antique satin
- 9 squares lace or doilies, 4×4 inches
- 1 yard fusible tricot interlining
- ⅔ yard lightweight fusible webbing
- Matching or monofilament sewing thread
- 16-inch polyester fiberfill pillow form

Treasured bits of antique lace, crochet doilies, eyelet, or cutwork can be preserved and beautifully displayed in this unique windowpane pillow. It's a quick and easy project that's sure to become a beloved heirloom.

Dimensions: 16 square inches

1. Iron fusible tricot to back of medium-weight fabric. Iron fusible webbing to back of lace squares. Remove paper backing.

2. From medium-weight fabric, on straight of grain, cut six 2×4-inch strips, two 2×13½-inch strips, two 2½×13½-inch strips, two 2½×18-inch strips, nine 4-inch squares, and two 13×18-inch rectangles.

3. Fuse lace squares to fabric squares. Arrange in pleasing pattern of 3 squares by 3 squares.

4. Stitch together 3 rows of 3 lace squares each, with 2×4-inch fabric strips between squares. Join rows together with 2×13½-inch strips between rows, carefully maintaining alignment of squares and strips. Stitch 2½×13½-inch strips to either side of pillow top. Stitch 2½×18-inch border strips to top and bottom.

5. Fold 1 long edge of one 13×18-inch rectangle over ¼ inch and press. Fold over ¼ inch again and stitch along folded edge. Repeat for other 13×18-inch rectangle. Lay rectangles on a flat surface, overlapping finished edges to create 18-inch square for pillow back. Stay-stitch along overlapped edges.

6. Pin pillow top to back with right sides together. Mark centers of each side ½ inch from edge. Mark corners 1 inch from edge. Draw lines connecting centers and corners. This will counteract the tendency toward "rabbit ear" corners. Stitch along drawn lines around all 4 sides. Remove stay-stitching from pillow back, trim corners diagonally, and turn. Insert pillow form.

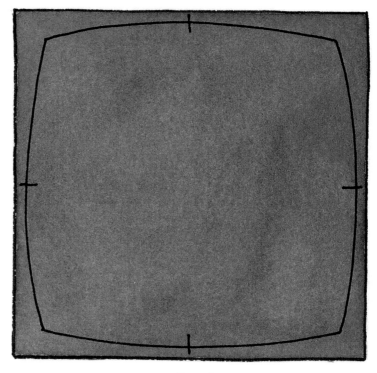

Step 6

COLONIAL HOUSE

 Easy

TEA SET

65

What You'll Need

1 yard light blue

1 yard rose print

½ yard light green

⅛ yard each or scraps dark green, light brown print, dark brown print, dark red, tan, and yellow for appliqués

2 yards fusible webbing

1½ yards fusible fleece

White dual duty thread

Dogwood, cloister brown, white, kerry green, red, and dark old rose rayon machine embroidery threads

2 packages white bias corded piping

1 skein pink 6-strand embroidery floss

5-inch length light blue satin ribbon, ¼ inch wide

11-inch length pink satin ribbon, ¼ inch wide

½ cup "simmering-type" potpourri

Polyester fiberfill

1¼-inch white button for each cozy or placemat

You don't have to live in one of the original U.S. Colonies to enjoy elegant Colonial style. With easy appliqués, this charming tea set is a breeze for anyone to make.

Dimensions: 12 ×18¼ inches, placemat;
14 ×12½ inches, cozy;
7½-inch circle, hot pad

The above quantities are sufficient for 1 tea cozy, 1 hot pad, and 2 placemats.

TEA COZY

1. Enlarge, trace, and cut out cozy pattern on page 71. Fold light blue fabric in half and place pattern with straight edge on folded fabric edge. Cut out full cozy pattern. Repeat to make another light blue cozy shape and 2 light green cozy shapes. Set aside green pieces and 1 blue piece.

2. From light green, cut one 3×14-inch strip. With right sides together, stitch to blue cozy piece 2½ inches from bottom edge. Open and press. Trim even with bottom edge of cozy and baste along edges. Trace and cut out all parts of house and tree patterns on pages 69 and 73. Iron fusible webbing to backs of appliqué fabrics. Place patterns facedown on paper side of fusible webbing, trace, and cut out. Remove paper backing. Transfer markings (indicated by dotted lines on patterns) to appliqué pieces. Arrange pieces on cozy front and fuse in place (see finished quilt illustration for placement). Using zigzag stitch and threads to match appliqués, machine stitch around all shapes except windows. For windows, use white thread, also stitching along marked lines.

3. For tree and bush, divide a length of floss into two 3-strand units. Using French knots, hand embroider where indicated on pattern.

4. Use pattern to cut 2 cozy pieces from fusible fleece. Fuse one fleece piece to the wrong side of each blue cozy piece. Stitch button to front door. Baste piping along curved edge of cozy front, with raw edge of piping even with raw edge of cozy piece. Stitch blue cozy pieces together, with right sides together. Clip curves and turn right side out.

5. Stitch green cozy pieces together with right sides together. Trim seam allowance close to stitching lines and leave wrong sides out. Slip green cozy unit over blue cozy unit, with right sides together and side seams and bottom edges aligned. Stitch along bottom edge, leaving 3-inch opening at back of cozy for turning. Turn right side out and push lining into cozy. Press. Stitch turning opening closed. Fold blue ribbon in half and hand stitch ribbon loop to top of cozy.

HOT PAD

1. Trace and cut out entire hot pad circle on page 72. From blue, cut 1 hot pad circle top. From green, cut 1 hot pad circle bottom. With right sides together, stitch green and blue together at straight edge to form complete circle. Open and press.

2. Trace and cut out tree pattern on page 73. Iron fusible webbing to wrong side of tree and trunk fabrics. Trace shapes on paper side of fusible webbing and cut out. Remove paper backing. Fuse tree pieces to center of circle. Add pink French knots to tree top. Zigzag stitch around appliqués with matching thread.

3. Cut full circle pattern from fleece and fuse to back side of blue and green circle. Baste piping around edges of hot pad front.

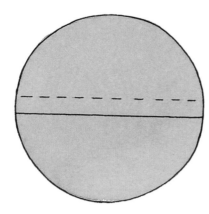

Step 4

4. From rose, cut 2 hot pad circle back pieces. Hem straight edges by turning under ¼ inch twice and stitching. With right sides together, lay half-circles over appliquéd circle with hemmed edges overlapping. Stitch half-circles to appliquéd circle. Clip curves, zigzag edges, and turn right side out.

5. For inner hot pad, cut 2 full circles from fabric of choice. Stitch circles together, leaving 3-inch opening. Clip curves and turn right side out. Stuff lightly with potpourri and fiberfill. Stitch opening closed. Insert into hot pad cover (remove potpourri pad before washing cover). Cut 4-inch length pink ribbon and fold in half. Hand stitch ribbon loop to top of hot pad. Make bow with remaining pink ribbon and hand stitch to top of hot pad to cover base of ribbon loop.

PLACEMAT

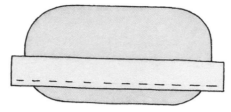

Step 1

1. Enlarge, trace, and cut out placemat pattern on page 70. For each placemat, fold blue fabric in half and place pattern with straight edge against folded fabric edge. Trace and cut out. Repeat to cut 1 full placemat from fleece and 1 from green. From green, cut one 3¼×17-inch strip. With right sides together, stitch to bottom of blue placemat shape with seam line ¼ inch from edge of green strip and 3 inches from bottom of blue shape. Open and press. Trim green strip to match shape of blue shape beneath it.

2. Trace and cut out all parts of house and tree patterns on pages 69 and 73. Iron fusible webbing to wrong side of appliqué fabrics. Place patterns faceup on paper side of fusible webbing, trace, and cut out. Remove paper backing. Fuse house, tree, and bush to placemat top. Embroider French knots on greenery. Follow instructions in step 2 of the tea cozy to stitch around appliqués.

3. Fuse fleece to wrong side of placemat top. Baste piping around edges of placemat top. Stitch blue top to green backing with right sides together, leaving 3-inch opening at bottom for turning. Clip curves and turn right side out. Press. Stitch button to door. Stitch opening closed.

Enlarge pattern at 125%
Grid method: ⅘ inch=1 inch

Placemat

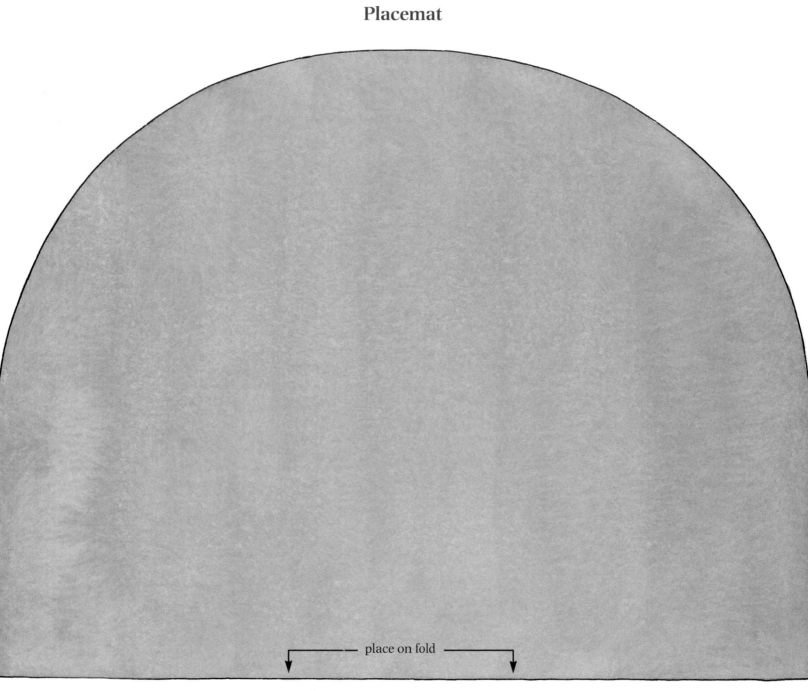

place on fold

Enlarge pattern at 150%
Grid method: ⅔ inch=1 inch
(Or copy from 1-inch grid to 1½-inch grid.)

Tea Cozy

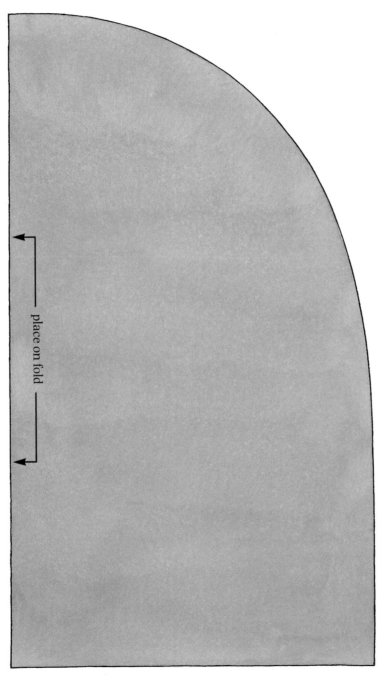

place on fold

Enlarge pattern at 200%
Grid method ½ inch=1 inch

Hot Pad

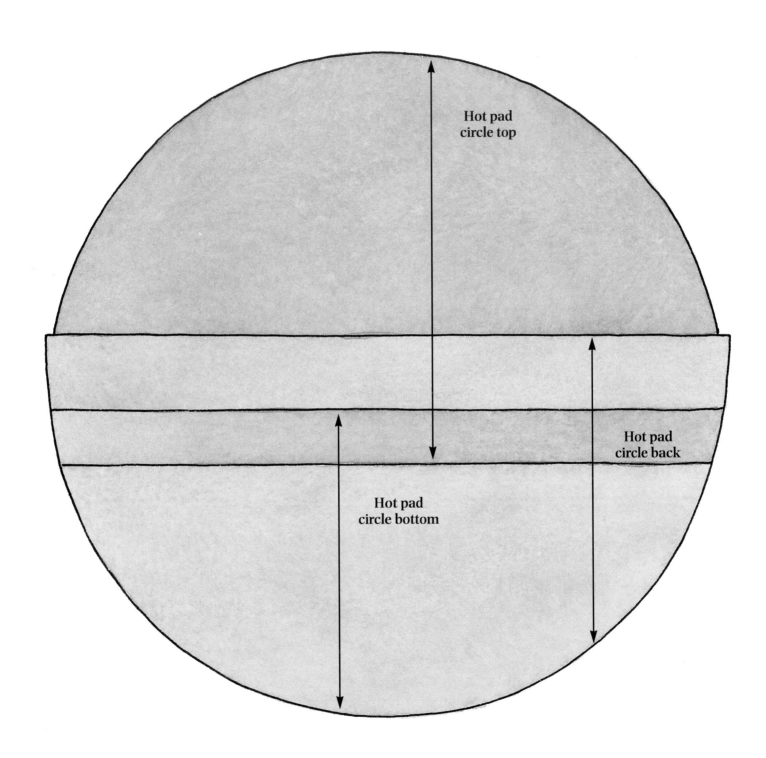

Hot pad
circle top

Hot pad
circle back

Hot pad
circle bottom

CASUAL
SOPHISTICATION

 Easy

TABLE SET

74

What You'll Need

⅔ yard each 2 coordinated patterns of mudcloth or other ethnic print fabrics, 45 inches wide

1⅔ yards terra cotta linen-weave cotton, 45 inches wide

1⅔ yards black linen-weave cotton

Medium-loft batting

3 yards fusible webbing

Monofilament sewing thread

Black rayon embroidery thread

Handwoven African mudcloth and neutral solid linen-weave cottons are paired to produce these ethnically inspired table linens. The table runner and placemats will lend international elegance to any setting.

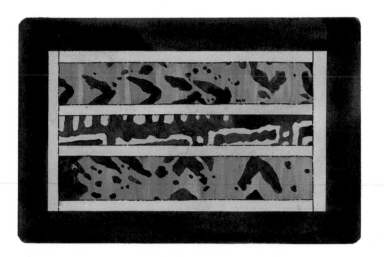

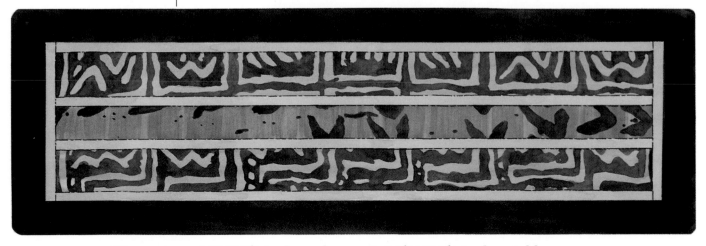

Dimensions: 18×12½ inches, placemat; 12½×36½ inches, table runner

Prewash all fabrics to test for colorfastness. Press and fold fabric lengthwise with selvages together. Measure and cut fabrics across the grain. The above quantities are sufficient for four placemats and a table runner.

PLACEMAT

1. For each placemat, cut one 3½-inch-wide strip of each mudcloth print. We will refer to these as print A and print B. From these, cut two 15-inch strips of each print. For each placemat you will need 3 strips of mudcloth. If you make 4 placemats, use 2 strips of print A and 1 of B for 2 of the placemats, then 2 strips of B and 1 of A for the other 2 placemats.

2. From terra cotta, cut two 1¾-inch-wide strips. From these, cut four 15-inch strips and two 9¼-inch strips. Fold each in half lengthwise with right sides facing out, and press. From remaining terra cotta, cut one 18½×13-inch rectangle.

3. From black, cut three 2½-inch-wide strips. From these, cut two 15-inch strips, four 13-inch strips, and two 18½-inch strips.

4. From batting, cut one 18½×13-inch rectangle.

Step 5

5. Carefully matching raw edges, stitch 15-inch folded terra cotta strip to right side of print A strip along long sides, stitching both edges of folded strip. Sandwich another 15-inch folded terra cotta strip between other long side of print A strip and print B strip (with right sides together) with all raw edges aligned. Stitch. Repeat for other long edge of print B strip, another terra cotta strip, and another print A strip. To remaining raw edge of print A strip, stitch folded terra cotta strip, stitching both edges of folded strip. Press all terra cotta strips toward center. See finished quilt illustration to make sure you are stitching strips in correct sequence.

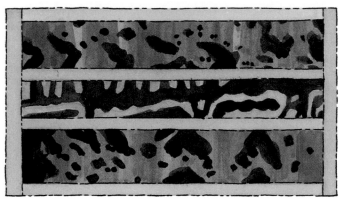

Step 6

6. Pin and stitch 9¼-inch terra cotta strips to sides of placemat, aligning raw edges and stitching both edges of folded strips. Press toward center.

7. With right sides together, stitch 15-inch black strips to top and bottom of placemat. Press. Stitch 13-inch black strips to sides of placemat and press.

Step 8

8. Iron fusible webbing to remaining black strips and remove paper backing. Fuse around outer edges of terra cotta rectangle, beginning with 18½-inch strips and overlapping 13-inch strips at corners. Using black thread and zigzag stitch, machine stitch around appliqué edges.

9. Place front and back panels with right sides together and batting underneath front. Stitch around all 4 sides, rounding corners slightly and leaving 4-inch opening in center of 1 long side. Trim excess fabric from corners, turn, and press. Hand stitch opening closed.

TABLE RUNNER

1. Follow same procedure as for placemats, but cut fabrics as follows: From print A, cut two 3½×33-inch strips. From print B, cut one 3½×33-inch strip. From terra cotta, cut four 1¾×33-inch strips, two 1¾×9¼-inch strips, and one 37×13-inch rectangle. From black, cut two 2½×33-inch strips and two 2½×13-inch strips for front and two 2½×37-inch strips and two 2½×13-inch strips for back. From batting, cut one 37×13-inch rectangle.

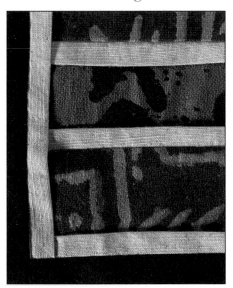

STARS & STRIPES FOREVER

 Easy

LAP QUILT & COASTERS

What You'll Need

Lap Quilt

1 yard red print

1¼ yard tan print

⅛ yard each of 8–12 different
plaids

1 yard blue print

½ yard solid red

2 yards backing fabric

50×65-inch piece cotton batting

¾ yard fusible webbing

Yellow rayon machine
embroidery thread

Off-white and dark red sewing
machine thread

Coasters

For 8 coasters:

⅛ yard plaid

⅛ yard blue

⅛ yard red print

⅛ yard tan print

⅛ yard fusible webbing

10×20-inch piece cotton batting

Yellow rayon machine
embroidery thread

Off-white and dark red sewing
machine threads

It's time to cuddle up with a good book
and a mug of hot cocoa! With this
matching set, you can create the perfect nook
for warming up on a cold winter's day.

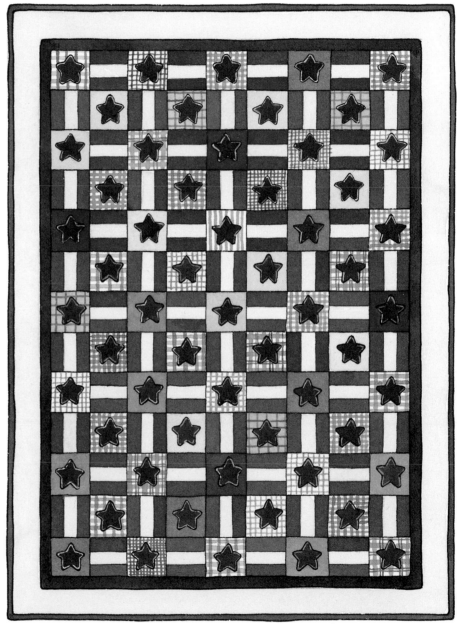

Dimensions: 45×60 inches, quilt;
4-inch square, coasters

79

LAP QUILT

1. Trace and cut out star pattern on page 81. Iron fusible webbing to wrong side of blue fabric and trace star 59 times on paper side of fusible webbing. Cut out stars and remove paper backing.

2. Cut six to eight 4½-inch squares from each plaid fabric, for a total of 59 squares. Fuse 1 star in the center of each plaid square.

3. Thread sewing machine with yellow rayon machine embroidery thread and off-white thread in bobbin. Using blanket stitch (2.5W-2.5L), stitch around stars. Pull threads to back and knot.

4. From red print, cut fourteen 1¾×45-inch strips. From tan print, cut seven 2×45-inch strips.

5. Stitch 1 red strip to either side of each tan strip lengthwise. Repeat for all strips. This makes 7 strip sets. Press seams toward red strips. Cut strip sets into 4½-inch units, making 58 strip units.

6. Stitch blocks together as shown in finished quilt illustration. Start by making horizontal rows, then stitch rows together vertically. Press.

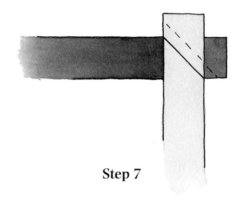

Step 7

7. From remaining blue fabric, cut five 1½×45-inch strips. With right sides together, place two strips at right angles with ends together. Draw a diagonal line from corner to corner where strips cross. Stitch on line and trim away excess ¼ inch from seam. Open and press. Repeat to add another strip. Cut this long strip in half and stitch to sides of quilt. Stitch remaining 2 strips to top and bottom of quilt. Press seam allowance to one side and trim excess.

8. From tan print, cut five 3½×45-inch strips. If necessary, stitch together as in step 7.

9. Measure quilt vertically through center. From tan print, cut 2 outer border strips to this length and stitch to sides. Measure quilt horizontally through the center and cut 2 strips to this length from tan print. Stitch to top and bottom. Press seams toward outer border.

10. Layer back, batting, and top and baste. If machine quilting, pin baste with one pin in the center of each square. With red thread, quilt in ditches between squares and around borders.

11. From red print, cut five 2½×45-inch strips. Stitch together as in step 7 for long sides. Follow directions in introduction to stitch binding to quilt.

COASTERS

For a really fast project, use 4½-inch plaid squares for the backs of the coasters, instead of bar units.

1. Trace and cut out star pattern on page 81. Iron fusible webbing to wrong side of blue fabric and trace star 8 times on paper side of fusible webbing. Cut out stars and remove paper backing.

2. Cut eight 4½-inch squares from plaid fabric. Fuse 1 star in center of each plaid square.

3. Thread sewing machine with yellow rayon machine embroidery thread and off-white thread in bobbin. Using blanket stitch (2.5W-2.5L), stitch around stars. Pull threads to back and knot.

4. From red print, cut two 1¾×45-inch strips. From tan print, cut one 2×45-inch strip. Stitch 1 red strip to either side of tan strip lengthwise. Press seams toward red strips. Cut strip set into eight 4½-inch units.

5. Cut batting into eight 4½-inch squares. Layer one square batting, one bar unit right side up on top of batting, and one star square right side down on top of bar unit. Pin at corners. Repeat for 7 remaining coasters.

6. Using walking foot, machine stitch through all 3 layers about ¼ inch from raw edges. Stitch around all 4 sides, leaving an opening to turn.

7. Turn all squares right side out. Stitch openings closed.

8. With red thread on plaid side and off-white on bar side, quilt around all squares ¼ inch from outside edges.

VASE OF LILIES

 Moderate

BED QUILT

What You'll Need

3 yards white-on-white print

1¾ yards green print

2 yards burgundy print with stripes and other motifs

¼ yard solid light rose

¾ yard medium rose print

¼ yard dark rose print

¼ yard dark brown print

2 yards light fusible webbing

1 package light fusible strip webbing, ¼-inch roll

4½ yards backing fabric

1 package medium-loft cotton or polyester batting

Rose, green, and dark brown threads to match appliqués

4 packages old rose double-thick bias quilt binding

3 packages jungle green double-fold bias tape

This quilt is reminiscent of the fine appliqué designs of the middle to late 1800s. With late-twentieth-century techniques you can make this elegant bedroom centerpiece in a weekend!

Dimensions: 75×82 inches

1. From white-on-white print, cut one 33½×41-inch rectangle, two 7½×47½-inch strips, two 7½×55-inch strips, and four 7½-inch squares.

2. From green print, cut (on lengthwise straight grain) two 7½×33½-inch strips, two 7½×41-inch strips, and eight 7½-inch squares.

3. Trace and cut out all pattern pieces on pages 86–87. Cut ¼-yard piece fusible webbing and iron to wrong side of remaining green fabric. Trace leaf pattern 35 times onto paper side of fusible webbing and cut out. Remove paper backing.

4. From burgundy print, cut two 7½×61½-inch strips and two 7½×69-inch strips.

5. Cut two ¼-yard pieces fusible webbing. Iron side by side to wrong side of solid light rose. Trace lily bud 6 times and bow 8 times onto paper side of fusible webbing. Cut out and remove paper backing.

6. From medium rose print, cut four 2×45-inch strips on the cross grain. Trim 2 strips to 33½ inches and 2 strips to 41 inches. From trimmed ends, cut four 2-inch squares. Cut equal-length pieces from fusible webbing roll. Iron to edges of wrong side of each strip and square. Remove paper backing.

7. Cut two ¼-yard pieces fusible webbing. Iron side by side to wrong side of remaining medium rose. Trace full lily pattern 19 times onto paper side of fusible webbing and cut out. Remove paper backing.

8. Cut one ¼-yard piece fusible webbing. Iron to wrong side of dark rose. Trace partial lily pattern 6 times onto paper side of fusible webbing. Cut out and remove paper backing.

9. Cut 12×17-inch piece fusible webbing. Iron to wrong side of dark brown. Trace vase pattern 5 times onto paper side of fusible webbing and cut out. Remove paper backing.

10. From backing fabric, cut two 2¼-yard pieces.

11. From green bias tape, cut one 24-inch length, two 70-inch lengths, eight 7-inch lengths, and two 60-inch lengths. Cut equal-size lengths from fusible webbing roll and iron to back of bias tape. Remove paper backing.

12. Place 33½×41-inch white-on-white rectangle on large flat ironing surface. Center vase 14 inches above bottom edge. Assemble 3 full lilies, 2 partial lilies, 2 lily buds, and 3 leaves, and pin in place as shown in finished quilt illustration. Pin top full lily 12 inches from fabric top. Slip a piece of green bias tape (from 24-inch length) under each flower and under edge of vase. Fuse, removing pins just prior to fusing.

13. Using finished quilt illustration for placement, assemble 1 bow, two 7-inch pieces green bias tape, 2 full lilies, and 2 leaves on each corner of center section. Bow ends should be 2 inches from each side, and lilies should be 2½ inches from side and 12 inches from corner point. Pin all motifs in place. Fuse.

14. Center equal-length 2-inch medium rose strip on each green strip and fuse. Center and fuse medium rose square on each of 4 green squares.

15. Place light rose bow diagonally on each remaining green square ⅝ inch from all edges and fuse.

16. Place brown vase diagonally on each white square so vase handles are ⅝ inch from sides, and top and bottom of vase are 3 inches from corners.

17. With a pin, mark center point of each 7½×55-inch white strip. Center and pin on 70-inch piece green bias tape, using finished quilt illustration as guide. Serpentine tape edges should be 1¼ inches from fabric sides, and tape ends should be 1¾ inches from long side edge. Trim tape ends even with fabric edges. For each strip, pin on 3 full lilies, 2 lily buds, and 8 leaves; referring to finished quilt illustration for placement. Strips should be identical. Fuse motifs and bias tape to strip.

18. In the same manner, center 60-inch bias tape pieces on 7½×47½-inch white strips. Pin 1 full lily, 2 partial lilies, and 4 leaves to each strip, using finished quilt illustration for placement. Strips should be identical. Fuse motifs and bias tape to strips.

19. Stitch longer green strips to sides of center panel. Lightly press seams toward green, keeping iron off fused appliqués and bias tape.

20. Stitch green square with medium rose square to each end of shorter green strips. Press seams toward squares. Stitch strips to top and bottom of center panel. Carefully press seams toward green.

21. Stitch longer white strips to sides of green. Stitch vase squares to shorter white strips, then pin and stitch to top and bottom of green. Lightly press seams toward white squares and strips.

22. Stitch longer burgundy strips to sides. Lightly press seams toward borders. Stitch bow square to each end of shorter burgundy strips and stitch to top and bottom of quilt.

23. Stitch together backing pieces to make 81×89-inch piece. Press seams open.

24. Layer quilt front, batting, and back and baste. Using zigzag stitch and matching thread, machine stitch around each lily, leaf, vase, and bow. Use straight stitch with matching green thread to stitch both sides of each piece of green bias tape. Zigzag stitch edges of medium rose strips and squares on green background. Follow manufacturer's instructions to stitch binding to quilt.

Leaf

Partial lily

Lily bud

Full lily

STRAWBERRY FIELDS

 Easy

BREAKFAST SET

What You'll Need

For each placemat:

¼ yard white

½ yard strawberry print

10×10-inch piece fusible
    webbing

13×17-inch piece batting

2 yards red rickrack

For hot pad:

¼ yard white

½ yard strawberry print

1 5-inch square fusible webbing

11-inch square batting

For both:

⅛ yard each or scraps red and
    green pin-dot fabrics

Red all-purpose thread

Red and green machine
    embroidery threads

Water-soluble pencil

Strawberries for breakfast—what a treat!
Start the day on a bright note with this perky
set. More than just a feast for the eyes,
this project is a snap to make!

Dimensions: 12×16 inches, placemat;
10×10 inches, hot pad

89

PLACEMAT

1. From white, cut one 8½×12½-inch rectangle. From strawberry print, cut four 2½×12½-inch strips and one 13×17-inch rectangle.

2. Trace and cut out strawberry and leaf patterns on page 91. Iron fusible webbing to wrong side of red and green pin-dot scraps. Trace 2 leaves, 3 berries, and 3 berry tops onto paper side of fusible webbing. Cut out and remove paper backing. Position on white as shown in finished quilt illustration. Fuse. Draw stem lines freehand with water-soluble pencil.

3. Using medium-width satin stitch and red and green machine embroidery threads, stitch around appliqués. With green thread, stitch over lines to make stems, and stitch a line about three-quarters of the way through leaf centers to create leaf veins.

4. Using all-purpose thread, stitch 1 strawberry print strip each to top and bottom of placemat. Stitch remaining 2 strips to sides. Press toward border.

5. Baste batting to wrong side of placemat top. Baste rickrack around front edges of placemat, aligning tips of one side of rickrack with raw edges of fabric. Stitch directly down center of rickrack. Trim away excess batting extending beyond edges.

6. With right sides together, stitch placemat front to strawberry print backing, leaving 4-inch opening along one side for turning. Clip corners and turn placemat right side out. Hand stitch opening closed. Press lightly.

7. Pin through fabric layers. Using red all-purpose thread, machine quilt in ditch around center block.

HOT PAD

1. From white, cut one 6½-inch square. From strawberry print, cut two 2½×6½-inch strips, two 2½×10½-inch strips, and one 11-inch square.

2. Trace and cut out strawberry and leaf patterns on page 91. Iron fusible webbing to wrong side of red and green pin-dot scraps. Trace 2 leaves, 2 berries, and 2 berry tops onto paper side of fusible webbing. Cut out and remove paper backing. Arrange on white as shown in finished quilt illustration. Fuse. Draw stem lines freehand with water-soluble pencil.

3. Using medium-width satin stitch and red and green machine embroidery threads, stitch around appliqués. Stitch over lines to create stems and stitch a line about three-quarters of the way through leaf centers to create leaf veins.

4. Stitch short strawberry print strips to top and bottom of hot pad and press toward border. Stitch longer strips to sides and press. Follow placemat steps 5 and 6 to complete hot pad. Using red all-purpose thread, quilt in ditch around center block, in border about ⅜ inch from center block, and in border about ¼ inch from outer edge.

5. Use remaining scraps of rickrack for bow and hanging loop. Tie a length of rickrack into bow and hand stitch to front of top left corner. Fold 6-inch length of rickrack in half and stitch to back of same corner to make hanging loop.

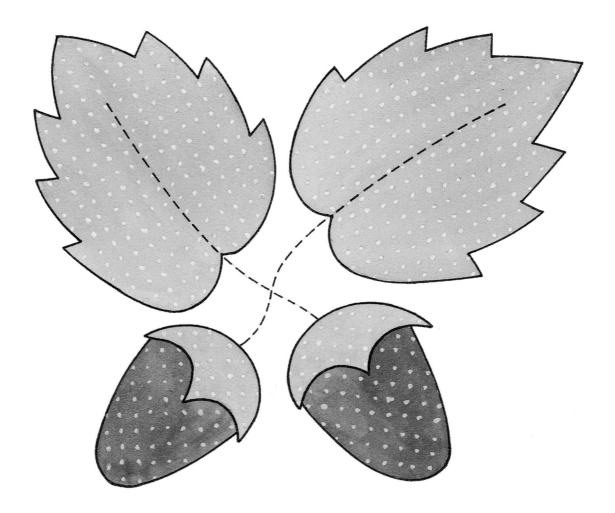

91

WHIMSICAL & WINSOME QUILTS

Who says you have to take your quilting seriously? Innovative concepts and playful designs make for wonderfully appealing quilts.

Here you will find a variety of whimsical approaches to quiltmaking. The Penguin Frolic and Guardian Angel baby quilts are sure to delight both little ones and their parents. The Southwest Cactus pillow brings in a lively touch of the desert, while the Underwater Fantasy wall hanging lets you make your own no-maintenance aquarium! The School Days wall hanging is a nostalgic look at days gone by. And, for more contemporary occasions, the Evening Glamour bag can be made in just the right colors to complement your favorite out-on-the-town outfit. These projects are as much fun to look at as they are to make!

92

PENGUIN FROLIC

 Moderate

BABY QUILT

What You'll Need

1 yard black solid

½ yard white-on-white print

2 yards white solid

1 yard bold black-and-white stripe print

1 yard black-and-white penguin print

3½ yards coordinating backing fabric

½ yard fusible webbing

2½ yards quilt batting, 54 or 60 inches wide

Tracing paper

Template plastic

Freezer paper

Penny

Glue

Pencil or chopstick

Black and white thread

12 tiny squeakers (optional)

It's believed that very small babies respond principally to black and white. Your favorite newborn will respond with pleasure to this exciting high-contrast quilt.

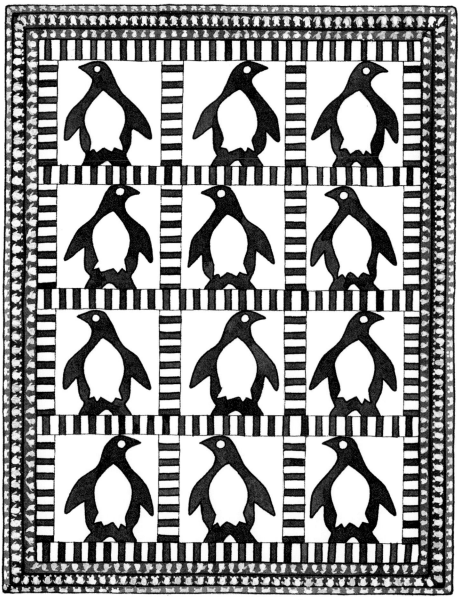

Dimensions: 50×64 inches

1. Enlarge pattern A (page 97) by 125%. Fold tracing paper in half and trace patterns A and B (pages 97–98), aligning center edge on fold. Trace penguin head C (page 98). Cut out. Place alignment line on head even with line on body; tape head in place. Glue penguin and piece B to template plastic and cut out.

2. Trace penguin onto freezer paper 12 times (6 with heads facing right, 6 facing left). Cut out. Iron freezer paper pieces to wrong side of black fabric. Cut out pieces, leaving ¼-inch margin of fabric outside penguin. Clip penguin at underarms and along curves.

3. Trace piece B 12 times on paper side of fusible webbing. Iron webbing to white-on-white. Cut out. For eye, trace penny 12 times onto paper side of fusible webbing. Iron to wrong side of white-on-white; cut out. Cut twelve 12½-inch squares from white.

4. From black-and-white stripe print, cut sixteen 2½×12½-inch strips for vertical sashes and five 2½×45-inch strips for horizontal sashes. From penguin print, cut six 3½×45-inch strips for borders and six 3½×45-inch strips for binding.

5. Press ¼-inch seam allowances under for all penguin bodies. Fold 12 white squares in half and press lightly to crease. Remove freezer paper from penguin and lay penguin on square, using center crease as guide. Head and feet will be near top and bottom of each square (at least ¼ inch away from each). Pin to square. Make 12.

6. Using black thread, machine stitch around edges of penguins, being careful that all edges are folded under. Remove paper from B pieces. Place on penguin, right side up. Center belly piece and fuse. With white thread in sewing machine set to satin or close zigzag, stitch around all edges.

7. Peel paper off 12 penny-shaped eye pieces. Place eye on each penguin and fuse. With white thread and satin stitch, stitch around all eyes.

8. Cut 2-inch slit in fabric behind belly appliqué—don't cut through white fabric! Stuff 5×5-inch square of batting, using pencil or chopstick, into slit. Push batting to edges of belly. If desired, insert tiny squeaker into each belly. Stuff all bellies, but don't sew slits shut. Lay out completed blocks in 4 rows of 3, using finished quilt illustration as guide.

9. Sew 12½-inch strip of black-and-white stripe print to right edge of each penguin block. Sew sashed blocks together into 4 horizontal rows of 3 blocks each. Sew remaining four 2½×12½-inch strips to left side of each row. Press seams toward sashes. Sew 45-inch strips of black-and-white stripe print to top of each 3-block row and to bottom of last row. Press seams toward sashes. Pin and sew 4 rows together.

10. Measure quilt from center top down to bottom edge. This is the measurement for borders of 2 long sides. Sew six 3½-inch strips of penguin print together end to end. Press seams in 1 direction. Cut 2 strips to measurement. Pin and sew strips to long edges. Press seams toward border. Measure from center of each long edge across to opposite edge. This is the measurement for top and bottom borders. Cut 2 strips to measurement. Pin and sew to quilt. Press seams toward border.

11. Cut 51×65-inch piece backing fabric. Layer quilt front, batting, and back and baste.

12. Quilt around outline of penguins and around outside of bellies and ¼ inch on inside of bellies. Echo quilt around penguin bodies, spacing quilt lines about ¾ inch from each other. For borders, trace penguin head pattern around borders in chalk and quilt. On striped borders, quilt along 1 edge of each black stripe.

13. From penguin print, cut six 3¾-inch strips for binding. Follow directions on pages 19–20 to stitch binding to quilt.

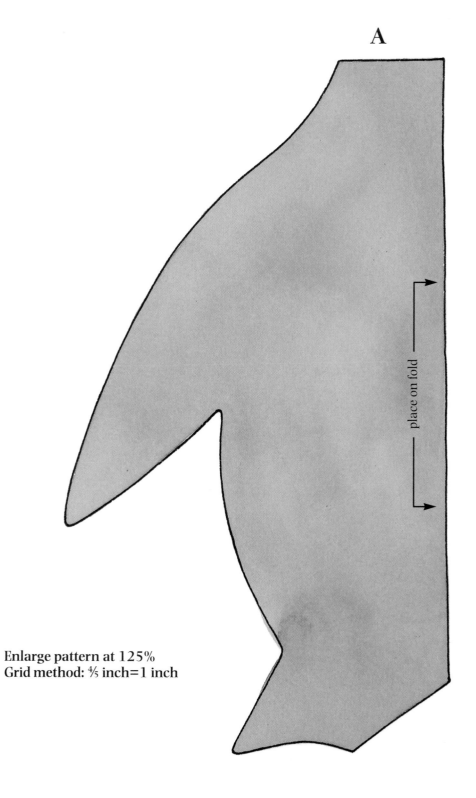

A

place on fold

Enlarge pattern at 125%
Grid method: ⅘ inch=1 inch

97

B

C

place on fold

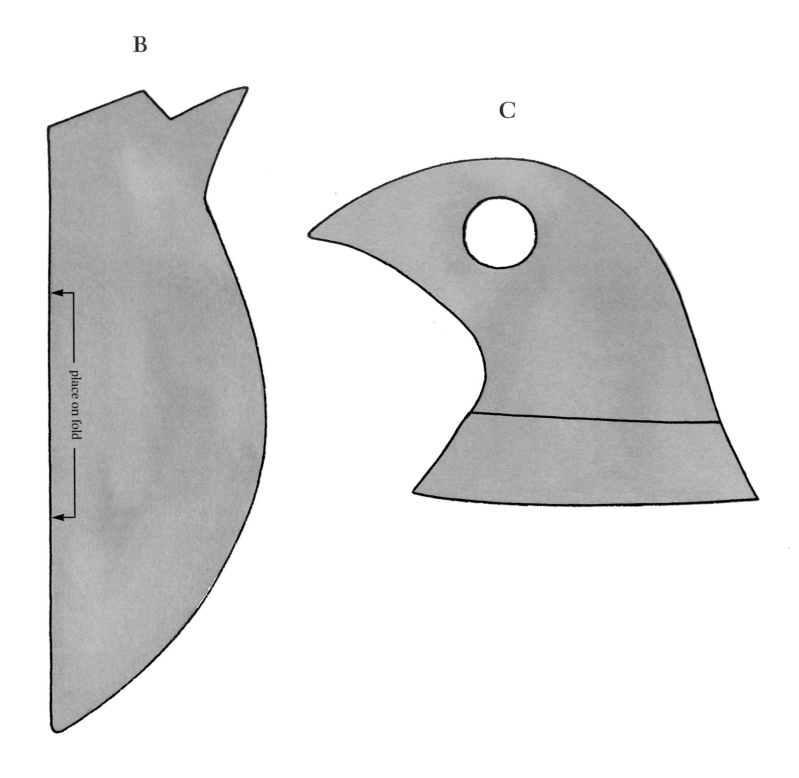

EVENING
GLAMOUR

 Easy

B A G

What You'll Need

⅔ yard each 4 or 5 textured ribbons in several widths, colors, and patterns, about 7 yards total

1 yard ribbon, 1½ inch wide, matching other ribbon colors

7×18-inch piece fusible tricot interfacing

7×18-inch piece soft woven or tricot fabric for lining

1⅓ yard rattail cording

Transparent monofilament thread

Gold rayon embroidery thread

Upholstery thread

Grid board

Press cloth

Safety pin or bodkin

It only takes some colorful ribbons and a few hours to make this stylish evening bag. Or choose delicate pastels and lace to make a trousseau keepsake bag for the bride-to-be.

Dimensions: 6×9 inches

100

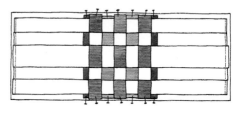

Step 1

1. Place fusible tricot on grid board with glue side up. Cut textured ribbons into lengths to cover tricot completely horizontally. Then cut and weave short pieces vertically beginning at center and creating a solid, symmetrical pattern. While weaving, pin ends of ribbons to grid board to prevent shifting. Carefully place press cloth over ribbons and fuse. Remove pins. Stay-stitch around outer edges ¼ inch from cut edges to secure loose ends of ribbons.

2. Thread machine with gold rayon embroidery thread. Center presser foot over ribbon edges and apply decorative stitches in continuous rows over all ribbon edges to create crazy quilt effect.

3. Fold in half with right sides together and sew ½-inch side seams. Trim away excess fabric and ribbon from seams, leaving ¼-inch allowance. Trim diagonally at corners. Turn.

4. Lay slightly more than 1 yard upholstery thread over 1-yard length of ribbon, with thread close to ribbon edge and extending beyond ribbon ends. Using transparent monofilament thread, zigzag stitch over upholstery thread, taking care to avoid catching thread in stitches. Gather ribbon to fit around upper edge of bag and sew ends together. Pin in place around upper edge of bag with right sides together. Baste. Stitch all the way around bag using ½-inch seam allowance.

5. To make lining, fold lining fabric in half with right sides together and sew side seams, leaving opening on one side to turn. Slip bag inside lining with right sides together and stitch around upper edge, leaving ½-inch seam allowance. Ruffle should be between bag and lining. Turn. Press ruffle up.

6. To make casing, stitch around upper edge of bag through all layers ½ inch from top and again ½ inch below first row of stitching. Open seams of lining between stitching rows.

7. To make drawstring, thread rattail cording through casing using safety pin or bodkin. Tie ends together in double knot and arrange rattail to extend equally from both ends of casing. Pull out lining and hand stitch opening. Push lining back into bag.

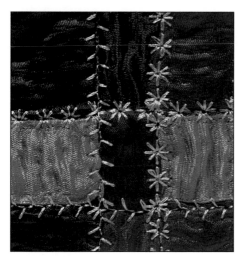

UNDERWATER FANTASY

 Easy

WALL HANGING

102

What You'll Need

½ yard light blue print

¼ yard multicolored print

¼ yard each dark green, purple, peach, dark blue, turquoise, red, and gold prints

Threads to match all fabrics

¼ yard ultra-hold fusible webbing

⅝ yard backing fabric

¼ yard medium blue print

18¾×26¾-inch piece quilting fleece

11 black or brown poms, 5mm

16-inch length red yarn

Tacky glue

Making this wall hanging is almost like creating your own aquarium!
The motifs are composed of appliqués and easy-to-make fabric yo-yos, a popular quilting technique of the early 1900s that's back in style.

Dimensions: 20×28 inches

Hint: Instead of making your own yo-yos, you can purchase premade ones in fabric or craft stores.

1. From light blue print, cut 14×22-inch rectangle. From multicolored print, cut two 3½×45-inch strips. Cut 1 strip into two 22-inch pieces and the other into two 20-inch pieces.

2. Trace and cut out all pattern pieces on pages 105–106. Cut 9×6-inch piece fusible webbing and iron to wrong side of peach. Trace large coral pattern onto paper side of fusible webbing. Turn pattern piece over and trace 1 small reversed coral piece. Cut out corals.

3. Cut 9×11-inch piece fusible webbing and iron to wrong side of dark green. On paper side of fusible webbing, trace 1 large plant, 1 small plant, and 1 reversed small plant. Cut out.

4. Using large circle pattern, trace and cut out the following circles: 8 dark green, 11 purple, 8 peach, 11 dark blue, 12 turquoise, 14 red, and 12 gold. Using medium circle pattern, trace and cut out the following circles: 2 dark blue and 2 gold. Using small circle pattern, trace and cut out 4 peach circles.

5. From backing fabric, cut 21×29-inch rectangle. From medium blue print, cut three 2×45-inch strips for binding.

6. Line up coral and plants on light blue print background. Left end plant should be ¾ inch from left side and ⅞ inch from bottom. Large coral piece should be 7¼ inches from left side and 1⅛ inches from bottom. Large plant should be 5 inches from right side and 1⅞ inches from bottom. Small coral should be 3⅝ inches from right side and 1½ inches from bottom. Right end plant should be ½ inch from right side and 1⅛ inches from bottom. Fuse appliqués.

7. With right sides together, stitch 22-inch multicolored strips to top and bottom of light blue. Press seams toward strips. Stitch 20-inch multicolored strips to sides. Press seams toward strips.

8. Make each circle into a yo-yo. Thread a needle with strong matching thread. Knot ends together so thread is double. Turn edge of circle under ¼ inch toward inside around circle and hand gather as close to folded edge as possible. Pull thread tightly and knot. Press flat to form circle with gathered edge on 1 side.

9. For purple sea anemones, fold yo-yo in half with stitched side on outside bottom. Make 3 of these.

10. For octopus, pull large dark blue yo-yo center outward. Thread large needle with red yarn and pull through stitched end 4 times. Cut yarn ends each to 2 inches in length to make 8 tentacles.

11. Each fish is a combination of anemone and octopus techniques. Sew octopus yo-yo and anemone yo-yo of same color together with matching thread at stitched ends. Make the following large fish: 1 dark blue, 2 turquoise, 3 red, and 2 gold. Make 1 dark blue and 1 gold medium fish.

12. Attach yo-yo motifs to background with tacky glue or hand stitch with needle and thread. Refer to finished quilt illustration for placement or design your own seascape. Attach small peach yo-yos to coral tips.

13. Place 8 yo-yos of each color with stitched side up around inner part of multicolored border. Our quilt uses the following order, starting at top left corner and going right: dark green, red, dark blue, gold, purple, turquoise, and peach. Firmly glue or stitch yo-yos in place.

14. Layer quilt front, fleece, and back and baste. Follow directions on pages 19–20 to stitch binding to quilt. Glue pom eyes to octopus and fish.

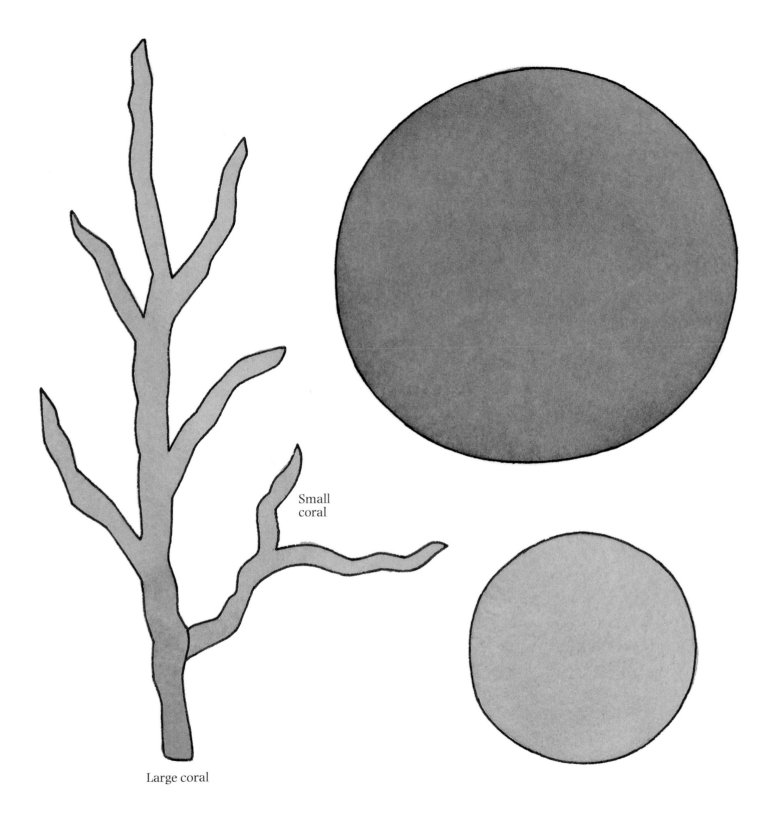

Small
coral

Large coral

106

S O U T H W E S T
C A C T U S

 Easy

P I L L O W

What You'll Need

½ yard green sueded cotton

½ yard golden brown sueded cotton

1¼ yards low-loft polyester batting

1 bag polyester fiberfill

Fabric stabilizer

Green rayon embroidery thread

Monofilament thread to match golden brown fabric

Tracing paper

Air soluble marker

Softened earth tones and sueded cotton fabrics set the warm Southwestern tone. This pillow invites a light desert breeze to blow through any room.

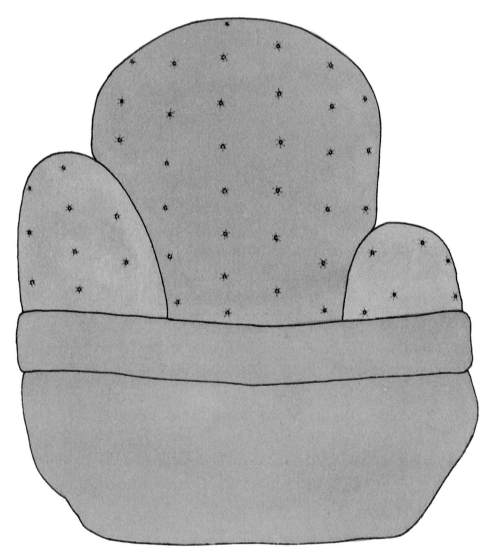

Dimensions: approximately 16×14 inches

1. Enlarge cactus pattern on page 110 by 125 percent. Fold tracing paper in half and place over pattern with fold lined up with straight side of pattern. Trace pattern on 1 side of tracing paper and cut out. Open and trim off 1 side as indicated by closely spaced dotted line on pattern. Fold green in half with right sides together, trace pattern on wrong side of fabric, and cut out 2 cactus pieces.

2. Use pattern piece to cut 2 pieces batting to same dimensions as green. Place each green piece right side up on a batting piece with fabric stabilizer underneath. With green rayon embroidery thread, machine stitch small star-shaped motifs about 1 inch apart to simulate cactus texture.

3. Remove fabric stabilizer, place quilted layers with right sides together, and stitch, leaving lower edge open. Trim seams, clip curves, and slash points. Turn right side out. Transfer topstitching lines using air soluble marker.

4. Enlarge pot pattern on page 111 by 200 percent. Fold golden brown fabric with right sides together. Trace pattern on wrong side and cut out two pots. With right sides together, stitch across both short sides, leaving lower center seam open for turning and stuffing. Fold down 2 inches along upper edge. From batting, cut 3×40-inch strip. Fold batting and stuff inside fabric fold. Stitch, leaving ½-inch seam allowance. This will be lip of pot.

5. Slip pot over cactus with right sides together, and match inside lip edge of pot with lower edge of cactus. Pin together, carefully matching side seams. Stitch together using ½-inch seam.

6. Turn right side out. Topstitch on cactus, following topstitching lines to create stuffing channels. Stuff with fiberfill, using pencil or paintbrush handle to distribute fiberfill into channels. Stuff pot firmly and hand stitch closed.

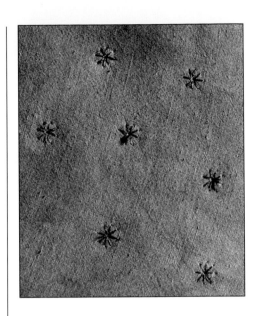

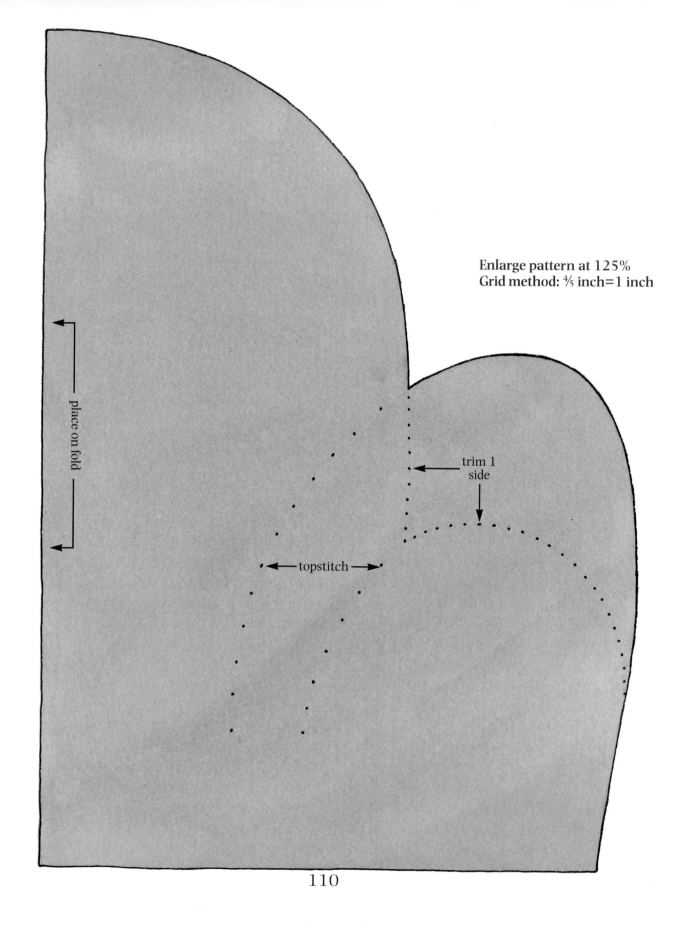

Enlarge pattern at 125%
Grid method: ⅕ inch=1 inch

place on fold

trim 1
side

←topstitch→

Enlarge pattern at 200%
Grid method: ½ inch=1 inch

GUARDIAN
ANGELS

 Moderate

BABY QUILT

What You'll Need

1 yard dark purple

¾ yard purple and pink print

⅝ yard lavender

⅝ yard white-on-white print

¼ yard gold

1¾ yards backing fabric

⅝ yard binding fabric

3½ yards white gathered lace, 1 inch wide

1 package low-loft polyester batting

White and gold threads

Your favorite little cherub will sleep soundly with these quilted angels keeping watch. With machine piecing, this stunning project is easier than it looks!

Dimensions: 41×54 inches

1. Trace and cut out all patterns on page 115. From dark purple, cut twelve 5½-inch squares, seven 10¼-inch squares, and one 10½-inch square. Cut each 10¼-inch square in half diagonally, forming 14 triangles. Cut 10½-inch square along both diagonals, forming 4 triangles.

2. From purple and pink print, cut five 1½×45-inch strips and twenty-four 4¼-inch squares. Cut each square in half diagonally, making 48 triangles.

3. From lavender, cut four 1½-inch squares and sixteen 5⅝-inch squares. Cut each 5⅝-inch square in half diagonally, making 32 triangles.

4. From white-on-white, cut four 10¼-inch squares. Cut each square in half diagonally, forming 8 triangles. Cut eight 5⅝-inch squares. Cut each square in half diagonally, making 16 triangles. Trace around piece A 8 times onto white and cut out. Clip curves to dotted line.

5. On gold, trace 12 B pieces and 8 C pieces. Cut out. Clip piece B to dotted line at inner points. Clip curved side of piece C to dotted line. Cut eight 14½-inch pieces of gathered lace. Cut five 2×45-inch strips of fabric for binding.

6. Center and pin gold star on dark purple square with points toward corners of square. Turn under ¼ inch on each side and hand appliqué to purple with gold thread. Make 12.

7. Place and pin gold piece C on large dark purple triangle, keeping edges even at right angle. Baste close to edge on 2 sides. Fold under clipped edge and hand appliqué. Place white piece A on top of halo with edges even. Baste edges and hand appliqué onto halo. Make 8.

8. Stitch purple and pink print triangle to 4 sides of each purple star square. Stitch 2 opposite sides, then remaining sides. Press seams toward triangles. Trim points.

9. Stitch 3 lavender triangles and 1 white triangle to star square centers. Make 8. Stitch 2 lavender triangles (to top and bottom) and 2 white triangles (to sides) to star square centers. Make 4. Press seams toward outer triangles and trim points.

10. Machine baste lace to long side of each large white triangle. Pin and stitch 6 large white triangles to large purple triangles with angel heads and halos, making large squares.

11. Arrange squares and triangles into diagonal rows. (Refer to finished quilt illustration for placement.) Stitch blocks into rows, then join rows to form large rectangle. Trim 2 purple and pink strips even with top and bottom of quilt. Cut 1 border strip in half. Stitch each half strip to whole strip. Pin and stitch long border strip to each side of quilt. Trim ends. Press seams toward borders.

12. Stitch lavender square to each end of top and bottom border strips. Press seams toward squares. Pin and stitch these strips to top and bottom of center (don't catch lace). Press top seam toward border and bottom seam toward center.

13. Layer quilt front, batting, and back and baste. Hand quilt, starting at center. Quilt close to outside edge of each star and inside edge of each purple square and purple and pink print square. Quilt close to outside edge of each angel wing, halo, and skirt, and close to edge of remaining lavender and dark purple triangles.

14. Follow directions on pages 19–20 to cut binding and stitch to quilt.

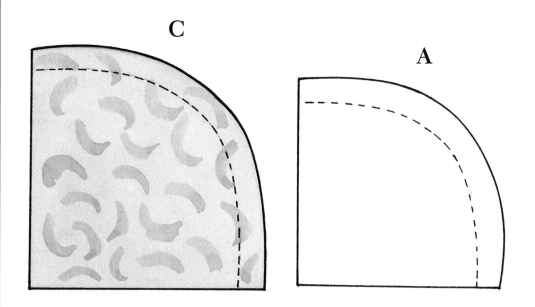

C

A

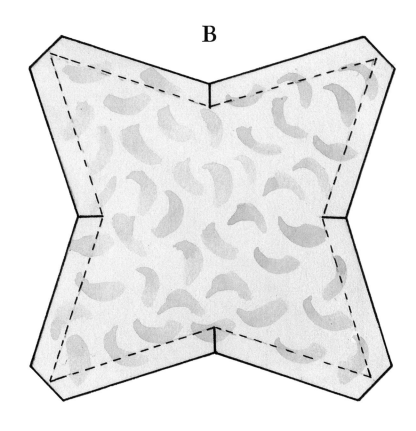

B

SCHOOL DAYS

 Moderate

WALL HANGING

What You'll Need

¾ yard white-on-white print

¾ yard red print

⅛ yard blue print

⅛ yard dark green print

⅞ yard backing fabric

½ yard dark blue print

30-inch square low-loft batting

Bell, 9mm

8-inch piece jute

½ yard fusible webbing

Transparent monofilament thread

Black thread

Appliqué fabrics:

⅛ yard brown print for tree

⅛ yard tan print for fence

⅛ yard dark brown print for door and window frames

Scraps: green for grass and apple leaves; red, white, and blue for flag; black for flagpole; light brown for flagpole top; gold for leaves; brown for cat; cream for steps; white print for windows; red for apples; white for apple highlights

School is just starting at this little red schoolhouse! Old-fashioned piecing techniques combine with appliqué to evoke the days of one-room schoolhouses. A perfect gift for your favorite teacher.

Dimensions: 28×26½ inches

This quilt will be cut and assembled in rows. As each row is completed, it should measure 17½ inches horizontally. The quilt will still work if your rows are not exactly 17½ inches, as long as the rows are all the same width.

1. Assemble first row. From white, cut two 5½-inch squares. From red, cut one 7½×5½-inch rectangle. Stitch one white square to each short side of red rectangle.

2. Assemble second row. From white, cut two 5×4½-inch rectangles and one 4⅞-inch square. From red, cut one 4⅞-inch square and one 2-inch square. Cut squares in half diagonally from corner to corner.

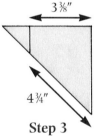

Step 3

3. Place right sides of white triangles together. Measure 3⅜ inches across 1 short side and lightly mark fabric at edge. Measure 4¾ inches along long side from point toward point nearest mark and make another mark at fabric edge. Cut from 1 mark to the other, cutting away a small triangle.

4. With right sides together, stitch short side of 2-inch red triangles to white shapes along edge where you cut away triangles. Press to background.

5. Stitch white/red triangles to 4⅞-inch red triangles along diagonals to form squares. Stitch squares together with red on inside and stitch 5×4½-inch white rectangles to either side.

6. Assemble third row. From white, cut two 7½×2-inch rectangles and one 2⅜-inch square. From red, cut one 2⅜-inch square.

7. Place right sides of 2⅜-inch squares together and draw diagonal line from corner to corner on wrong side of top fabric. Stitch together ¼ inch from line on either side. Cut on line and press open. Stitch resulting squares together with red on inside and stitch 7½×2-inch rectangles to either side.

Step 8

8. For row 4, cut one 17½×3-inch strip from white. Pin center of each row. Match centers and stitch together rows 1, 2, 3, and 4.

9. For inner border, cut two 1½×45-inch strips from blue. Measure through center of quilt horizontally and cut 2 strips to this length (about 17½ inches) from one precut strip. Stitch strips to top and bottom of quilt. Measure quilt vertically through center. Cut 2 strips of blue print to this length (approximately 15½ inches) from other precut strip. Stitch strips to sides of quilt.

10. For checkerboard border, cut three 1½×45-inch strips from green and three 1½×45-inch strips from white. Also cut one 1½×11½-inch strip from white and set aside. Stitch together 1 white and 1 green strip lengthwise. Press to dark. Repeat for other strips.

11. Cut sewn strips into 1½-inch sections. Stitch sections together end to end, making strips of alternating colors. Make 2 strips of 19 squares beginning and ending with green. Make 3 strips of 19 squares beginning and ending with white. Make 2 strips of 4 squares beginning with white and ending with green.

12. Refer to finished quilt illustration as you stitch borders to quilt. For top of checkerboard border, stitch short checkerboard strips to ends of 1½×11½-inch white strip, with green squares next to white strip. Stitch to 19-square strip that begins and ends with green, and stitch border to top of quilt.

13. Stitch together lengthwise one 19-square strip beginning and ending with white and one 19-square strip beginning and ending with green. Stitch to bottom of quilt. Add one 19-square strip beginning and ending with white to each side of quilt.

14. For outer border, cut four 4×45-inch strips from red. Measure quilt horizontally through center. Cut 2 strips to this length from precut strips and stitch to top and bottom of quilt. Measure quilt vertically through center and cut 2 strips to this length from precut strips. Stitch to each side of quilt.

15. Trace and cut out all patterns on pages 120–121. Iron fusible webbing to back of all appliqué fabrics. Trace patterns on paper side of fusible webbing, cut out, and remove paper backing. From cream for steps, cut one ⅜×3⅜-inch rectangle and one ⅜×2½-inch rectangle. From black for flagpole, cut one ¼×8-inch strip. From tan for fence, cut two ¼×5-inch strips. Arrange appliqués on quilt as shown in finished quilt illustration and fuse.

16. Layer top, batting, and back and baste. Using transparent thread, machine quilt around edges of all appliqués and in ditches around schoolhouse and between borders. Quilt diagonal grid pattern in checkerboard border. Insert jute through top of bell and tie a simple bow. Hand stitch to bell tower. From black thread, cut eight 8-inch lengths. At midpoint of lengths, stitch to top of flagpole, taking several stitches through all three layers to secure. From black thread, cut ½-inch lengths. At midpoint of lengths, stitch to cat face to make whiskers. Take several stitches through all three layers to secure.

17. From dark blue print, cut four 3¼×45-inch strips. Follow directions on pages 19–20 to stitch binding to quilt.

Enlarge pattern at 125%
Grid method: ⅘ inch=1 inch

QUILTS FOR ALL SEASONS

Celebrate the arrival of each season with festive decorations. You can usher in spring, summer, fall, and winter with these exciting seasonal quilts.

You'll want to leave up the Simply Elegant Trees and Folk-Art Yuletide wall hangings all winter. The Happy Holidays card holder is a great way to treasure holiday wishes. When spring creeps in, the Brightly Blooming Tulips pillow is a hint of garden colors to come. The Americana Summer table runner celebrates the Fourth of July in all-American colors. In fall, the Country Pumpkin Patch and Fall Patchwork wall hangings will bring back warm autumn memories. Don't wait for a holiday—every season is a reason to decorate!

122

HAPPY HOLIDAYS

 Easy

Quilts for All Seasons

CARD HOLDER

124

What You'll Need

7⅞×10⅞-inch piece stiff cardboard

⅜ yard dark green print

¼ yard straw-colored print

⅛ yard or scraps Christmas fabric

⅛ yard or scraps lightweight fusible webbing

⅜ yard cotton flannel

Thread to match or contrast with fabrics

2 yards dark red grosgrain ribbon, ¼ inch wide

Chalk marking wheel

Here's a way to treasure the expressions of cheer and goodwill that fill your home at Christmastime. This card holder gives you a handy and festive spot to keep your favorite holiday cards and letters.

Dimensions: 8×11 inches

1. Select images from Christmas fabric for decorations. Cut a piece of fusible webbing slightly larger than each image selected and iron to wrong side of fabric. Cut out each image and remove paper backing.

2. From dark green, cut two 9×12-inch rectangles. From straw-colored print, cut two 8-inch squares. From cotton flannel, cut one 9×12-inch rectangle and one 8-inch square. From ribbon, cut one 13-inch length and two 10-inch lengths. (Remaining ribbon can be used to decorate designs as desired.)

Step 3

3. Center cut-out design on right side of one 8-inch straw-colored square. Fuse. Arrange ribbon around design edges and topstitch in place.

4. Cover decorated pocket piece with other straw-colored square, placing right sides together. Add 8-inch cotton flannel square on top. Stitch around edges, using ½-inch seam allowance and leaving 3-inch opening for turning.

5. Trim seam allowance to ¼ inch and clip across corners, taking care not to cut into stitching. Turn right side out and press. Slip-stitch bottom edge closed. Quilt around design as desired.

6. Place pocket on top of right side of one 9×12-inch dark green rectangle. Position pocket with 1 inch of green fabric on either side and below it. Center another Christmas design in space above pocket, remembering that outer ½ inch of green fabric is seam allowance.

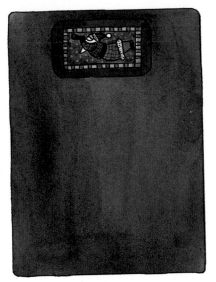

Step 7

7. Fuse upper design in place. Set pocket aside. Arrange ribbon around edges of upper design and topstitch in place.

8. Place decorated green piece on top of 9×12-inch cotton flannel rectangle. Quilt around design as desired.

Step 9

9. Reposition pocket as before and stitch around sides and lower edge. Backstitch at each upper corner.

10. With right sides together, place plain 9×12-inch dark green rectangle on top of decorated piece. Stitch ½-inch seam from one lower corner, up side, across top, and down other side to lower corner. Trim side and top seam allowances to ¼ inch. Clip across top 2 corners, taking care not to cut into stitching.

Step 11

11. Turn right side out and press. Fold under ¼ inch at each end of 13-inch ribbon length. Arrange ribbon on back of background panel at upper corners. Tack ribbon in place by stitching back and forth.

12. On upper corners of cardboard, mark spots ¾ inch from corners down sides and across top. Trim upper corners of cardboard by cutting through marked points. Insert cardboard in fabric pocket. Fold under seam allowances along bottom edge of card holder and slip-stitch closed. Stitch center of 10-inch ribbon length to each upper corner and tie each ribbon in a bow.

SIMPLY ELEGANT TREES

 Easy

WALL HANGING

128

What You'll Need

¼ yard green print

¼ yard dark red print

¼ yard white-on-white print

⅛ yard brown

½ yard Christmas print

¾ yard backing fabric

⅓ yard dark green

30-inch square low-loft polyester batting

Gold metallic thread

Red and green threads to match fabrics

"Elegant" is just the right word for this holiday wall hanging. Rich colors and gold accents create an aura of sophisticated charm.

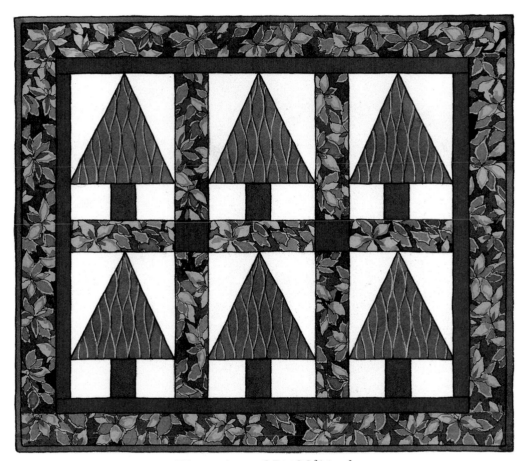

Dimensions: 27 × 23¾ inches

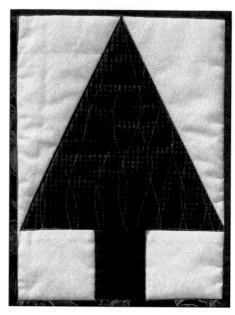

Step 1

1. With metallic thread, sew embellishing lines on green print fabric from top to bottom. Lines should be graceful curves and may intersect each other.

2. Trace and cut out all pattern pieces on page 131. Trace and cut six A triangles from green print. Cut six B triangles and six B reversed from white-on-white. Sew triangle B and triangle B reversed to each triangle A to form tree.

3. From brown, cut six 2×2½-inch trunks. From white-on-white, cut twelve 2½×2¾-inch rectangles. Sew 2 white rectangles to either side of each brown trunk, along 2½-inch sides. Sew trunk sections to bottom of tree sections to form blocks.

4. Cut two 2½×45-inch strips from Christmas print. Cut strips into four 8-inch strips and three 6-inch strips. Cut two 2½-inch squares from dark red print.

5. Stitch together 2 rows of 3 trees each separated by Christmas print sashing and corner blocks. See finished quilt illustration.

6. Cut three 1½×45-inch strips from red print. Measure quilt vertically through center and cut 2 strips to this length from 1 of the long strips. Stitch to sides. Measure quilt horizontally through center. Use remaining strips to make border for top and bottom.

7. Cut three 2½×45-inch strips from Christmas print. Measure quilt vertically through center and cut 2 strips to this length from 1 of the long strips. Stitch to sides. Use remaining strips to make border for top and bottom.

8. Layer top, batting, and back and baste. Quilt in ditches around trees with gold thread. Quilt in ditches around blocks and borders with red thread. Cut three 2¾×45-inch strips from dark green. Follow directions on pages 19–20 to stitch binding to quilt, using green thread.

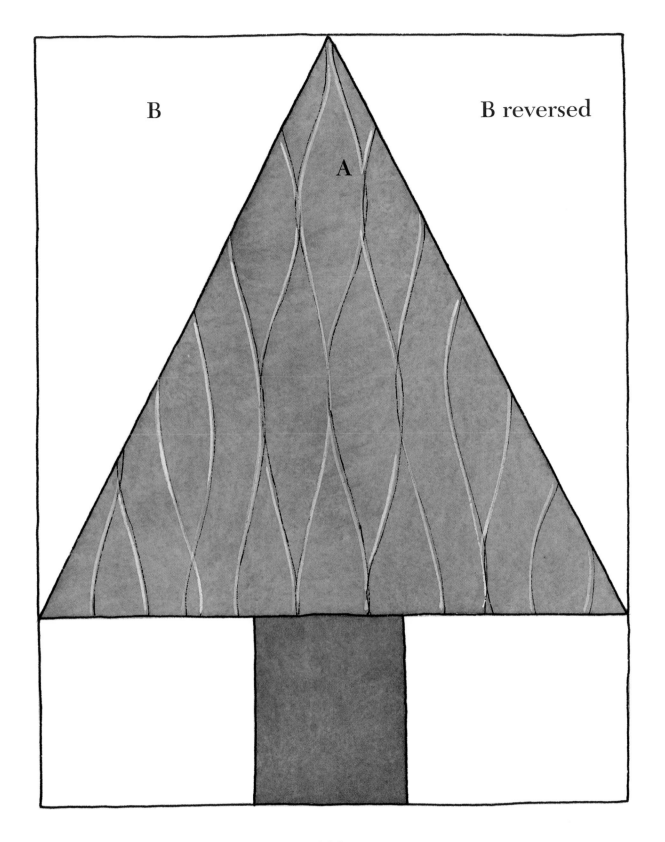

B

B reversed

A

131

FOLK-ART
YULETIDE

 **Difficult**

WALL HANGING

132

What You'll Need

Large Quilt

¼ yard tan print for house background

⅛ yard each 4 assorted prints for houses

⅛ yard each or scraps 4 assorted prints for roofs

Scraps 3 assorted prints for doors and chimney

9-inch squares each 3 tan prints for moose backgrounds

10-inch square tan print for snowman background

10-inch square tan print for mittens background

¼ yard brown print for tree background

⅛ yard or scraps tan print for checkerboard

⅛ yard green print

⅛ yard or scraps yellow print

⅛ yard or scraps orange print

⅛ yard or scraps dark brown print

⅓ yard black and tan print

⅛ yard black print

⅜ yard medium blue print

⅓ yard dark blue print for binding

1 yard backing fabric

38×32-inch piece low-loft batting

1 yard fusible webbing

9 assorted buttons

5 small red buttons

White and black threads

Red fine-point permanent marker

continued on page 134

Welcome the holidays country-style with these folk-art wall hangings. Traditional country colors and piecing methods blend seamlessly with contemporary design and appliqué techniques.

Dimensions: 36×30 inches, large quilt; 10½×20½ inches, small quilt

What You'll Need, continued:

⅛ yard white for snowman

⅛ yard each or scraps 3 assorted prints for windows

⅛ yard each or scraps 3 brown prints for moose

⅛ yard red plaid for mitten

⅛ yard light blue plaid for mitten

Scraps: brown for stars; orange for snowman nose; assorted colors for snowman hat, patch, scarf, chimneys, mitten bands, and doors

Small Quilt

8½×9½-inch rectangle tan print for snowman background

8½×7½-inch rectangle tan print for mitten background

⅛ yard dark red print

16 1½×2-inch scraps in various colors for scrappy border

⅛ yard dark blue print

⅓ yard backing fabric

12×32-inch piece low-loft batting

¼ yard fusible webbing

17 buttons in assorted sizes and colors

Red fine-point permanent marker

White and black threads

Appliqué fabrics:

⅛ yard white for snowman

⅛ yard red print for mitten

⅛ yard blue print for mitten

Scraps: orange for snowman nose; assorted colors for scarf, hat, patch, mitten bands, and mitten stars

These quilts use the techniques known as bias rectangle and template-free angle piecing. See page 49 for directions.

LARGE QUILT

1. Assemble tree unit. From tree background, cut ten 4½×1½-inch rectangles, ten 2×1-inch rectangles, six 2×5-inch rectangles, and five 2⅞-inch squares. From green print, cut five 2⅞-inch squares. From dark brown print, cut five 1½×1-inch rectangles.

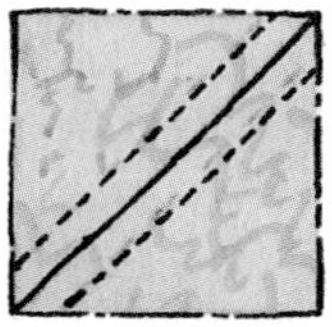

Step 2

2. Place one 2⅞-inch background square and one 2⅞-inch green square with right sides together. Draw diagonal line from corner to corner. Stitch ¼ inch on each side of line. Cut apart on line. Repeat for rest of 2⅞-inch squares. Press half the squares toward green and the other half toward background. Pair squares so that green sides are together, forming tree tops. Pair up opposing seams. Stitch and press to one side.

3. Stitch 2×1-inch tree background piece to either side of each tree trunk, along 1-inch sides. Join tree and trunk units to form five 4½×3-inch blocks. Add one 4½×1½-inch background piece to top and bottom of each tree block. Stitch tree blocks together in a row, with 2×5-inch background pieces between tree blocks and at each end of row. Press and set aside.

4. The houses are numbered 1 through 3 from left to right. **Church:** From house background, cut one 6×3-inch rectangle, one 3⅜-inch square, and one 1×6-inch rectangle. From church fabric, cut one 5½×3½-inch rectangle and one 3⅜-inch square. (You may prefer to use different fabrics for church base and church roof.) **House 1:** From house background, cut one 6½×2-inch rectangle, two 2×2½-inch rectangles, and two 5×4-inch rectangles. From house 1 fabric, cut one 4½×8½-inch rectangle. From roof 1 fabric, cut two 2×2½-inch rectangles and one 3½×2½-inch rectangle. **House 2:** From house background, cut one 6×3-inch rectangle and one 2×1½-inch rectangle. From house 2 fabric, cut one 6×3-inch rectangle and two 2¾×2-inch rectangles. From roof 2 fabric, cut one 5×2-inch rectangle and one 2×1½-inch rectangle. From door 2 fabric, cut one 1½×2-inch rectangle.

House 3: From house background, cut one 2×1½-inch rectangle, one 3½×1½-inch rectangle, one 2½×1½-inch rectangle, and one 2×2½-inch rectangle. From house 3 fabric, cut one 4×1½-inch rectangle, one 2×1½-inch rectangle, and one 1½-inch square. From roof 3 fabric, cut one 3½×1½-inch rectangle and one 1½-inch square. From chimney fabric, cut one 1×1½-inch rectangle. From door 3 fabric, cut one 1½-inch square. **Star:** From house background, cut one 4½×1½-inch rectangle, four 1½×2½-inch rectangles, four 1½-inch squares, one 4½×3-inch rectangle, and one 1½×8-inch strip. From orange print, cut eight 1½-inch squares. From yellow print, cut one 2½-inch square. **Moose:** From moose background fabrics, cut two 7-inch squares and one 7½×7-inch rectangle. **Inner border:** From black print, cut one 20½×1-inch strip.

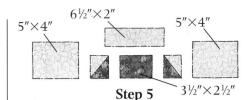

Step 5

5. The houses will be pieced in sections. Start with section 1. Make 1 right and 1 left bias rectangle with 2×2½-inch background and house 1 roof pieces. Following diagram, stitch section 1 together (5×4-inch background pieces were cut with house 1).

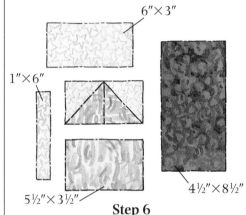

Step 6

6. Assemble section 2. Place one 3⅜-inch background square and one 3⅜-inch church square with right sides together. Draw diagonal line from corner to corner and stitch ¼ inch on either side of line. Cut apart on line and press to dark. Stitch together with roof sides together to form church roof. Assemble church as shown in diagram and add house 1 rectangle to right side.

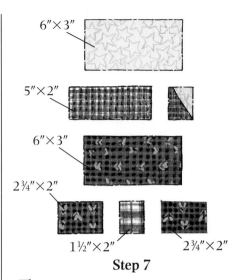

Step 7

7. Make section 3. Make 1 right bias rectangle using 1½×2-inch roof 2 and background rectangles. Assemble section 3 as shown in diagram.

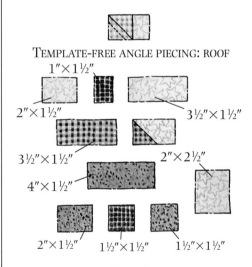

TEMPLATE-FREE ANGLE PIECING: ROOF

Step 8

8. Make section 4. Using template-free angle piecing technique, join 1½-inch roof 3 square to 2½×1½-inch background piece. Assemble section 4 as shown in diagram.

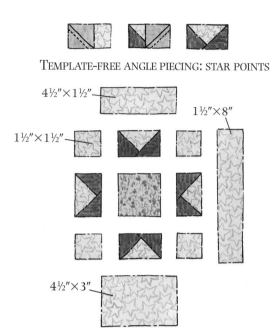

TEMPLATE-FREE ANGLE PIECING: STAR POINTS

4½"×1½"

1½"×8"

1½"×1½"

4½"×3"

Step 9

9. Assemble star. Using template-free angle piecing technique, stitch 1½-inch orange print squares to 1½×2½-inch background pieces. Assemble star as shown in diagram, adding background pieces.

10. Stitch moose background pieces together with 7×7½-inch rectangle in center. Stitch 20½×1-inch inner border strip to top. Stitch star block to section 4. Stitch section 2 to section 3. Stitch section 1 to the top of sections 2 and 3 and add section 4 with star. Refer to finished quilt illustration for placement.

11. Assemble snowman and mitten blocks and borders. From snowman background fabric, cut one 8½×9½-inch rectangle. From mittens background, cut one 8½×7½-inch rectangle. From medium blue print, cut two 31½×3-inch strips and two 30½×3-inch strips. From black and tan print, cut one 19×1½-inch strip, one 8½×1½-inch strip, two 29½×1½-inch strips, two 25½×1½-inch strips, and four 1½×2-inch rectangles. From tan checkerboard fabric, cut four 1½×2-inch rectangles.

12. Stitch together 1½×2-inch black and tan print and light checkerboard rectangles along 2-inch sides, alternating colors. From top to bottom, stitch together checkerboard strip, snowman background rectangle, 8½×1½-inch black and tan print strip, and mittens background rectangle. Add 1½×19-inch black and tan print strip to left side of unit.

13. Stitch snowman and mitten block to right of house and moose block. Stitch tree block to top of quilt. See finished quilt illustration for placement.

14. Stitch 1½×29½-inch black and tan print strips to top and bottom of quilt. Stitch 1½×25½-inch black and tan print strips to each side of quilt. Stitch 31½×3-inch medium blue strips to top and bottom of quilt. Stitch 30½×3-inch medium blue strips to each side of quilt.

15. Trace and cut out all patterns on pages 138–140. Iron fusible webbing to wrong side of appliqué fabrics. Trace patterns on paper side of fusible webbing and cut out. Position on quilt as shown in finished quilt illustration and fuse. Sew buttons on mitten and snowman. Use black thread and basting stitch to make snowman mouth. Make French knots for snowman eyes and moose eyes. Use white thread to stitch around snowman patch. With fine-point permanent marker, draw snowman cheeks.

16. Layer front, batting, and back and baste. Using white thread, hand quilt around edges of appliqué shapes and in ditches around borders. Hand quilt lines radiating from star. To save time and create a different look, you can machine quilt instead. From binding fabric, cut four 3¼×45-inch strips. Follow directions on pages 19–20 to stitch binding to quilt.

SMALL QUILT

1. From snowman background, cut one 8½×9½-inch rectangle. From mitten background, cut one 8½×7½-inch rectangle. From dark red, cut two 1½×20½-inch strips and one 1½×8½-inch strip. From scrappy border fabrics, cut sixteen 1½×2-inch rectangles.

2. Stitch background pieces to 1½×8½-inch dark red strip along 8½-inch sides. Stitch scrappy border rectangles together along 2-inch sides to make 2 units of 8 rectangles each. Stitch units to top and bottom of quilt. Stitch 1½×20½-inch dark red strips to sides.

3. Trace and cut out snowman and mitten patterns on pages 139–140. Iron fusible webbing to wrong side of appliqué fabrics. Trace patterns on paper side of fusible webbing and cut out. Position on quilt as shown in finished quilt illustration and fuse. Use black thread and basting stitch to make snowman smile. For snowman buttons and eyes, make French knots with black thread. Use black thread to stitch around snowman patch. Layer front, batting, and back and baste. Using white thread, hand quilt around edges of scarf and hat appliqués. Using black thread, hand quilt around edges of snowman, snowman nose, mitten, and star appliqués. Hand or machine quilt in ditches around borders. Stitch buttons on scrappy border rectangles and mitten. From dark blue, cut three 3¼×45-inch strips. Follow directions on pages 19–20 to stitch binding to quilt.

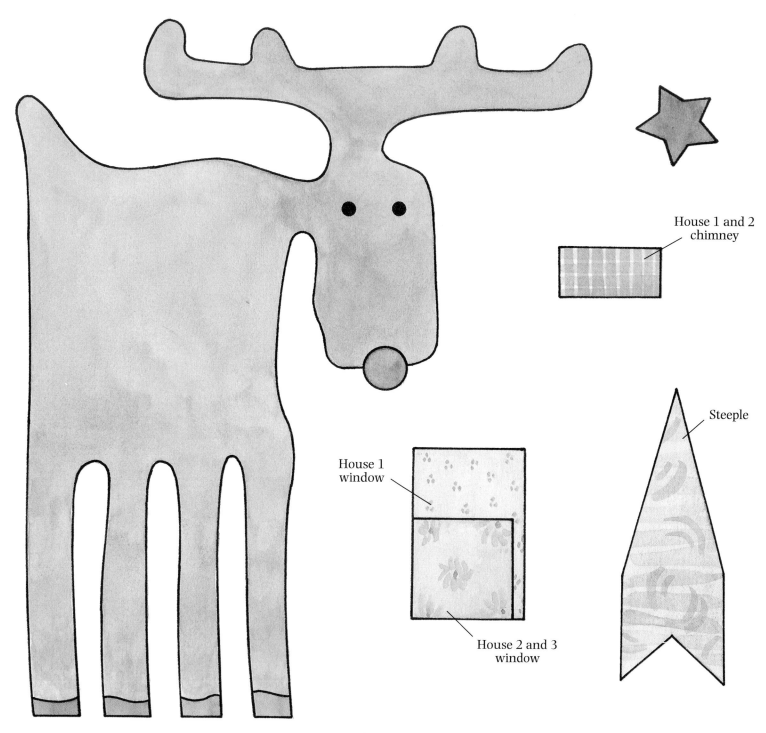

House 1 and 2
chimney

Steeple

House 1
window

House 2 and 3
window

138

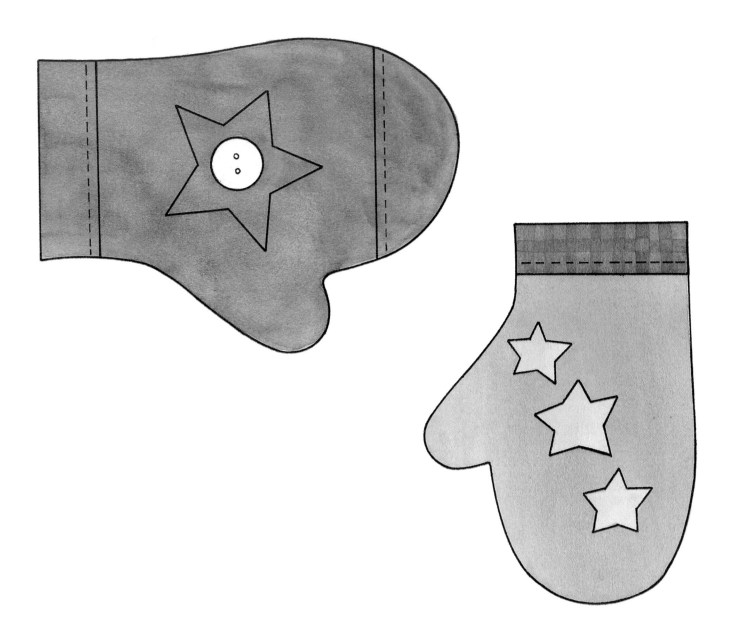

Brightly
Blooming Tulips

 Moderate

P I L L O W

What You'll Need

⅜ yard each yellow, red, orange, green, light blue, and dark blue sueded cotton fabrics

½ yard medium blue sueded cotton

2¼ yards cording, ½-inch wide

16-inch polyester fiberfill pillow form

Monofilament sewing thread

This springlike pillow will perk up any room. Dimensional appliqués add an interesting twist, and hand-colored sueded cotton fabrics give a soft but vibrant look.

Dimensions: 17-inch square

142

1. From light blue, cut one 12½×18-inch rectangle. From medium blue, cut one 6½×18-inch rectangle and two 13½×18-inch rectangles. From dark blue, cut two 3×44-inch strips. Stitch together end to end and cut to make 80-inch strip.

2. To make pillow front, stitch light blue rectangle to 6½×18-inch medium blue rectangle along long sides, using ½-inch seam allowance. For pillow back, fold 1 long edge of one 13½×18-inch medium blue rectangle ¼ inch and press. Fold over again and stitch. Repeat for other medium blue rectangle. With right sides up, lay dark blue rectangles on flat surface, overlapping finished edges to form 18-inch square. Stay-stitch across overlapped edges. Set aside.

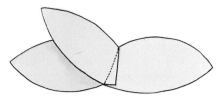

Step 3

3. Enlarge, trace, and cut out patterns on pages 144–145. Fold yellow and red fabrics in half with right sides together. Trace petal pattern on wrong side of yellow 3 times and wrong side of red 5 times. Leave at least ½ inch between shapes. Stitch on traced lines all the way around each shape and cut out, leaving ¼-inch seam allowance. Slash as marked on pattern and turn. Cut 1 yellow and 2 red petals in half. Fold remaining double petals in half along fold line marked on pattern. Insert half petal in center of each folded petal and stitch to secure at lower cut edge.

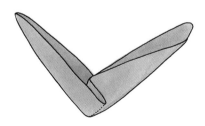

Step 4

4. Fold green in half with right sides together and make 5 leaves by the same method, using leaf pattern. To shape, fold in half lengthwise with slash to outside. Press. Fold along fold line. Stitch along lower portion of V shape.

5. From green, cut two 4×1-inch strips, one 7×1-inch strip, one 6½×1-inch strip, and one 3½×1-inch strip. Fold strips in half lengthwise, stitch, and turn.

6. With right sides together, fold orange fabric in half. Trace pot pattern on wrong side of fabric and stitch all the way around shape on traced line. Cut out, leaving ¼-inch seam allowance. Cut slit, turn, and press. Fold down upper lip of pot and fold up lower rim along fold lines as shown on pattern with slit to back. Press.

7. Arrange pot and flowers on pillow top. Cut stems to fit. Place leaves at base of stems along upper lip of pot. Invisibly hand stitch each shape in place, leaving leaf ends and dimensional parts of pot free.

8. Mark centers of each side of pillow back ½ inch from edge and corners 1 inch from edge. Draw a line to connect marks. This will minimize "rabbit ears" effect.

9. With right sides out, fold dark blue strip over cording and stitch close to cording using zipper foot. Pin cording along marked line on right side of pillow back, clipping seam allowance of cording at corners to fit. To finish ends of cording, open seams where cording ends meet, cut cording to fit together exactly, overlap seam allowances, and stitch back together to create continuous cording border. Stitch cording to pillow back. With right sides together, pin pillow front and back. Stitch around all 4 sides using zipper foot to get as close to cording as possible. Remove stay-stiching from pillow back and turn. Insert pillow form.

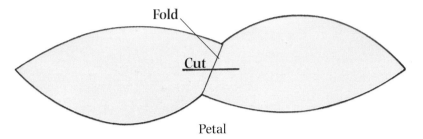

Petal

Enlarge pattern at 150%
Grid method: ⅔ inch=1 inch

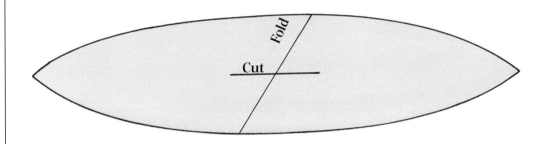

Leaf

Enlarge pattern at 150%
Grid method: ⅔ inch=1 inch
(Or copy from 1-inch grid to 1½-inch grid.)

Enlarge pattern at 125%
Grid method: ⅘-inch=1 inch

AMERICANA SUMMER

 Difficult

TABLE RUNNER

146

What You'll Need

⅞ yard cream print

½ yard white-on-white print

⅓ yard blue print

¼ yard green print

⅛ yard gold print for small star points

⅛ yard or scraps (1½-inch squares) gold print for small star centers

2×12-inch strip brown print

¼ yard light red print

½ yard dark red print

¼ yard dark blue print

22×48-inch piece batting

¼ yard fusible webbing

White and red threads

24 white buttons of various sizes

It's time to get out the flags and celebrate the Fourth of July! This all-American design, made with traditional quilting techniques, will give your home just the right patriotic touch. Use it as a wall hanging, too!

Dimensions: 20½×46½ inches

For this quilt you will use the template-free angle piecing technique. See page 49 for directions.

1. First, assemble flag. From cream print, cut one 1½×44-inch strip and one 8½×44-inch strip. From 1½×44-inch strip, cut two 1½-inch squares, one 1½×2-inch rectangle, three 1½×2½-inch rectangles, two 1½×3½-inch rectangles, one 1½×4½-inch rectangle, one 1½×5-inch strip, one 1½×5½-inch strip, and one 1½×6-inch strip. From 8½×44-inch strip, cut one 8½-inch square, one 6¼-inch square, one 1½×7-inch strip, and one 3½×14½-inch strip. From white-on-white print, cut two 1½×22-inch strips. From one of the strips, cut one 1½-inch square, one 1½×2-inch rectangle, one 1½×2½-inch rectangle, and two 1½×4-inch strips. From dark red print, cut two 1½×22-inch strips. From one of the strips, cut one 1½-inch square, two 1½×2-inch rectangles, one 1½×2½-inch rectangle, one 1½×3-inch rectangle, and one 1½×5-inch strip. From dark blue print, cut one 2½×22-inch strip. From this strip, cut one 2½×4½-inch strip, one 1½×3-inch rectangle, and one 1½×3½-inch rectangle.

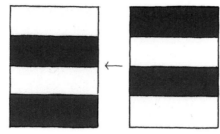

Step 2

2. With right sides together, sew dark red and white 1½×22-inch strips together lengthwise. Press to dark. Turn and cut into four 3-inch units. Sew units together with colors alternating to create a checkerboard effect.

3. Lay out rows as shown in diagram on page 149. Stitch together blue and cream horizontal rows on each side of dark red and white unit. Then stitch together vertical columns on each side of dark red and white unit. Stitch columns to sides of flag block. Stitch together remaining rows horizontally, then stitch all rows together vertically. Block should measure 12½×9½ inches.

4. Cut 8½-inch cream square in half diagonally. With right sides together and corners extending ¼ inch beyond flag block on each end, add one 8½-inch triangle to top of flag. Press to cream.

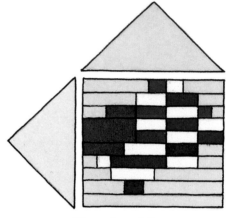

Steps 4 and 5

5. Cut 1½ inch off straight side (not bias) of remaining 8½-inch triangle. With right sides together and corners extending ¼ inch beyond flag block on each end, stitch to left side of flag. Press away from flag.

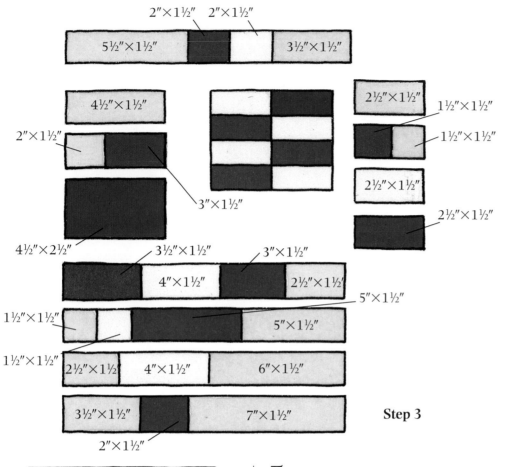

2"×1½" 2"×1½"

5½"×1½"   3½"×1½"

4½"×1½"

2½"×1½"   1½"×1½"

2"×1½"   1½"×1½"

3"×1½"

2½"×1½"

4½"×2½"

2½"×1½"

3½"×1½"   3"×1½"

4"×1½"   2½"×1½"

5"×1½"

1½"×1½"

5"×1½"

1½"×1½"   2½"×1½"   4"×1½"   6"×1½"

3½"×1½"   7"×1½"

2"×1½"

Step 3

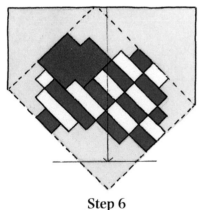

Step 6

6. Measure 12 inches down from top of flag block, and draw a horizontal line across bottom corner of flag block. Cut along line, cutting off a triangle. Stitch ⅛-inch seam across bottom to prevent bias from stretching.

7. Cut 6¼-inch cream square in half diagonally. With right sides together and corners extending ¼ inch beyond flag unit on each end, add 6¼-inch triangle to bottom left side of flag. Press away from flag.

Steps 7 and 8

8. From remaining 6¼-inch triangle, cut 1½ inches off straight side (not bias). With right sides together and extending ¼ inch beyond corner of flag unit on each end, stitch to bottom right side of flag. Press away from flag.

9. Trim flag block to measure 14½×12 inches. Take care not to stretch edges. Add 3½×14½-inch cream strip to flag bottom.

10. Cut 2×12-inch strip fusible webbing and iron to wrong side of brown print. Draw 1×12-inch rectangle on paper side of fusible webbing. Cut out and fuse to flag block. (See finished quilt illustration.) Finished flag unit should measure 14½×15 inches.

11. Assemble 3 small stars. From cream, cut one 1¾×44-inch strip. From this strip, cut twelve 1¾-inch squares and twenty-four 1-inch squares. From star point fabric, cut one 1¾×44-inch strip. From this strip, cut twenty-four 1¾×1-inch rectangles. From star center fabric, cut three 1½-inch squares.

149

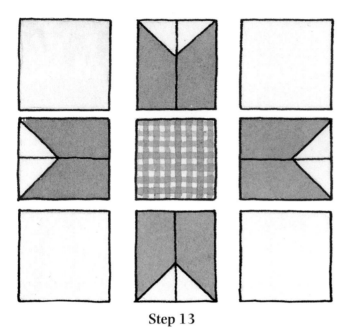

Step 13

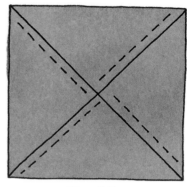

Step 15

Step 12

12. Using template-free angle piecing technique, with right sides together, stitch twelve 1-inch cream squares to twelve 1¾×1-inch star point pieces with angles going 1 direction. Stitch remaining 12 with angles going in the opposite direction. Press each set of 12 in opposite directions. Stitch star points together. Make 12 units.

13. Assemble 3 stars as shown in diagram. Each star should measure 4 square inches. Stitch star blocks together in a row.

14. Assemble large star. From cream, cut one 4⅞×22-inch strip and one 2×44-inch strip. From 4⅞×22-inch strip, cut one 4⅞-inch square and four 4-inch squares. From 2×44-inch strip, cut two 2×14½-inch strips. Cut one 4⅞ square each from dark red, light red, and blue. From white, cut one 4-inch square.

15. With right sides together, pair up 4⅞-inch dark red square with cream square, and light red square with blue square. Draw an X on wrong side of red squares, and sew ¼ inch from lines as shown in diagram. Cut apart on the drawn lines and press toward red. Join dark red/cream triangles to light red/blue triangles to form squares. Make 4. Units should measure 4 inches; trim if needed. Assemble large star block.

150

Step 16

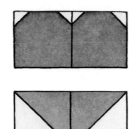

Step 19

16. Stitch the small stars to right side of large star block and add 2×14½-inch cream strips to top and bottom. Block should measure 14½×14 inches.

17. Assemble hearts. From cream, cut one 2⅞×44-inch strip, one 1½×44-inch strip, and one 1×44-inch strip. From 2⅞-inch strip, cut nine 2⅞-inch squares. From 1½-inch strip, cut six 1½×4½-inch strips. From 1×44-inch strip, cut thirty-six 1-inch squares. From green, cut one 2½×44-inch strip and one 2⅞×44-inch strip. From 2½-inch strip, cut seventeen 2½-inch squares. From 2⅞-inch strip, cut nine 2⅞-inch squares and one 2½-inch square. From light red, cut one 4×44-inch strip. From this strip, cut nine 4-inch squares.

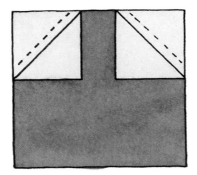

Step 18

18. With right sides together, using template-free angle piecing technique, stitch 1-inch cream squares to top corners of all 2½-inch green squares. Stitch 2 of these squares together side by side to form top of heart. Make 9.

19. Draw a diagonal line on wrong side of 2⅞-inch cream squares. With right sides together, pair 2⅞-inch cream squares with 2⅞-inch green squares. Stitch squares together ¼ inch on each side of line and cut on line. Open and press half to green and half to cream. Stitch 2 green/cream squares with opposing seams together with green in center. Make 9. Join the top and bottom heart units together. Hearts should measure 4½ square inches.

20. Stitch together 3 rows of 3 hearts each, with 1½×4½-inch cream strips between hearts. Each row should measure 14½×4½ inches.

21. Cut nine 4-inch squares fusible webbing and iron to wrong side of light red. Trace and cut out heart pattern below. Trace 1 heart pattern on paper side of fusible webbing in each square. Cut out hearts, remove paper backing, center on green hearts, and fuse. Blanket stitch around red heart centers.

22. Assemble quilt and borders. Stitch together quilt sections as shown in finished quilt illustration.

23. From blue print, cut three 1½×44-inch strips. From these strips, cut two 1½×16-inch strips and two 1½×40½-inch strips. From dark red print, cut three 3×44-inch strips. From these strips, cut two 3×21-inch strips and two 3×42-inch strips.

24. Stitch 1½×40½-inch blue strips to sides of quilt. Stitch 1½×16-inch strips to top and bottom. Stitch 3×42-inch red strips to sides of quilt. Stitch 3×21-inch strips to top and bottom.

25. Layer quilt front, batting, and back and baste. With white thread, machine quilt in ditches around borders. For a handmade look, hand quilt in ditches around shapes. With hand quilting, create shapes in red border and background and criss-cross pattern in flagpole. With red thread, hand quilt stars and other shapes in background and large star center. You may also use red thread to outline shapes quilted in border where they protrude into background. To save time, you may also quilt entirely by machine.

26. Cut four 2½×44-inch strips from dark blue print. Follow directions on pages 19–20 to stitch binding to quilt.

Heart

152

FALL
PATCHWORK

 Moderate

Quilts for All Seasons

WALL HANGING

What You'll Need

¾ yard cream print for scarecrow background and checkerboard

¼ yard cream print for cat background

¼ yard cream and gray print for fence background

⅛ yard cream print for pumpkin background

⅛ yard or scraps cream print for corner squares and side panels

⅛ yard each 6 fabrics for patchwork or scraps for 5 4½-inch squares

⅛ yard each 5 fabrics or 45 scraps in assorted medium to dark colors totaling $45 \times 1\frac{1}{2}$ inches for checkerboard border

⅝ yard backing fabric

⅓ yard dark brown print for binding

19×31-inch piece batting

1 yard fusible webbing

Raffia

Black fine point permanent ink pen

Red cosmetic powder blush

Cotton swab

Transparent monofilament thread

Black thread

Appliqué fabrics:

⅛ yard brown print for coveralls

⅛ yard black and tan check for shirt

⅛ yard orange print for pumpkins and cat's bow

continued on page 155

Fall in the country—leaves crackling underfoot, pumpkins waiting to be carved, a scarecrow in the fields! This wall hanging conjures up the nostalgic pleasures of autumn.

Dimensions: 18×30 inches

154

What You'll Need, continued

⅛ yard brown print for fence

⅛ yard black print for cat

Scraps: black for bats, brown for cat features, green check for rug, black print for rug, dark brown for hat, off-white for face and hands, assorted colors for patches, green for pumpkin leaves, brown for large pumpkin stems, green for small pumpkin stems

This quilt will be assembled in 5 sections, plus the border.

1. Assemble sections 1 and 2. From cat background, cut one 8¼×7¼-inch rectangle. From fence background, cut one 6¾×7¼-inch rectangle. Join rectangles along 7¼-inch sides with fence background piece to right.

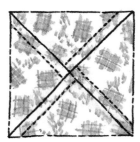

Step 2

2. Assemble section 3. Cut six 4¼-inch squares from patchwork fabrics. Match up 3 pairs of squares with right sides together. Draw an "X" on back of lighter fabric, with diagonal lines going from corner to corner. Stitch ¼ inch to right of each line from outside edge to intersecting drawn line. Cut on "X." Each square will make 4 half-triangle sets. Press seams to 1 side.

3. Pair up half-triangle sets with right sides together and stitch to create squares. Pair up different triangle sets to create patchwork look. Press seams to 1 side. Stitch all 5 squares together, end to end. Press seams up.

4. Assemble sections 4 and 5. From scarecrow background, cut one 11⅜ ×16⅛-inch rectangle. From pumpkin background, cut one 14½×4⅛-inch rectangle. Stitch section 3 (patchwork) to section 4 (scarecrow background) along 16⅛-inch sides, with patchwork to left. Press toward scarecrow background. Stitch sections 3 and 4 to section 5 (pumpkin background) along 14½-inch sides with pumpkin background at bottom. Stitch sections 1 and 2 to top of sections 3 and 4. Press seams up.

5. Assemble checkerboard border. From scarecrow background, cut five 45×1½-inch strips. From medium to dark checkerboard fabrics, cut five 45×1½-inch strips. From corner square fabric, cut six 2½-inch squares and two 4½×2½-inch rectangles.

6. For checkerboard, stitch 1 medium to dark strip to each scarecrow background strip lengthwise. Cut strips into 1½-inch sections. Assemble 4 checkerboard strips, each 11 squares long. Mix fabrics to create patchwork look, and make sure each strip begins and ends with dark squares on top, light squares on bottom. Make 4 checkerboard strips 6 squares long. Two should start with dark and end with light squares on top and start with light and end with dark squares on bottom. Two should start with light and end with dark squares on top and start with dark and end with light squares on bottom.

7. Stitch long checkerboard strips to ends of each 4½×2½-inch corner square rectangle. Stitch short checkerboard strips to opposite sides of two 2½-inch corner squares. Add one 2½-inch square to each end of top and bottom checkerboard strips. See step 8 diagram for correct orientation of light and dark checkerboard squares.

Step 8

8. Stitch long checkerboard borders to sides of quilt. Sides beginning and ending with dark squares should be toward inside. Stitch short checkerboard borders to top and bottom of quilt. Sides beginning and ending with dark checkerboard squares should be toward inside.

9. Trace and cut out all patterns on pages 157–161, enlarging where necessary. Iron fusible webbing to wrong side of fabrics for all appliqués. Trace patterns on paper side of fusible webbing, cut out, and remove paper backing. From fence fabric, cut one ¾×4¾-inch strip for bottom rail, three ¾×2⅜-inch strips for center fence slats, and two ¾×½-inch pieces for upper fence rails. Remove paper backing. Position all shapes on quilt as shown in finished quilt illustration. Cut several short lengths of raffia and position at scarecrow's wrists, ankles, neck, and head, just under edge of coverall appliqué. Fuse all appliqués, including raffia in bond around outer edges of coveralls and hat. Use black marker to draw facial features on scarecrow, pumpkin vines, leaf veins, and lines on pumpkins. Draw small, simulated stitches around pumpkins, pumpkin leaves, and scarecrow face. Rub tip of cotton swab against blush until some blush clings to swab. Place tip of swab on left side of scarecrow face and twist against fabric to make cheek. Repeat for right cheek. If you plan to wash the quilt, you might prefer to use red paint for cheeks.

10. Layer front, batting, and back and baste. With transparent thread, machine quilt in ditches around background blocks, borders, and patchwork triangles. Machine quilt around edges of all appliqué shapes. With black thread, machine quilt about ⅛ inch in from edge of coveralls and hand stitch around coverall patches. Cut three 3½×45-inch binding strips. Follow directions on pages 19–20 to stitch binding to quilt.

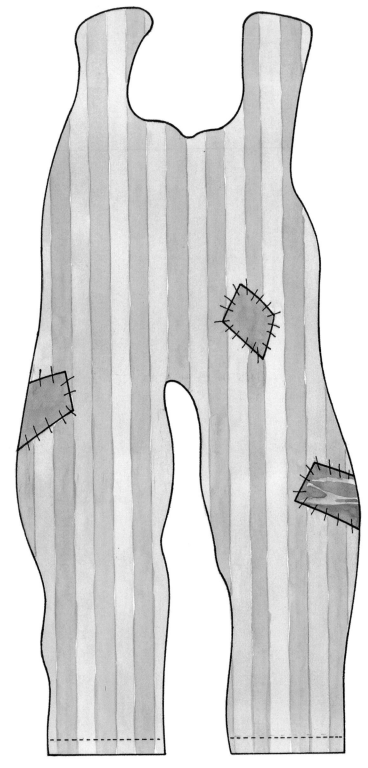

Enlarge pattern at 125%
Grid method: ⅕ inch=1 inch

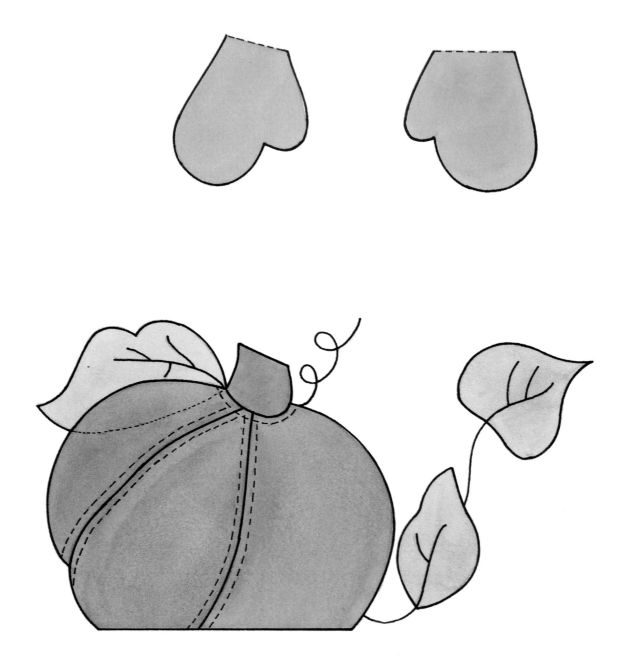

160

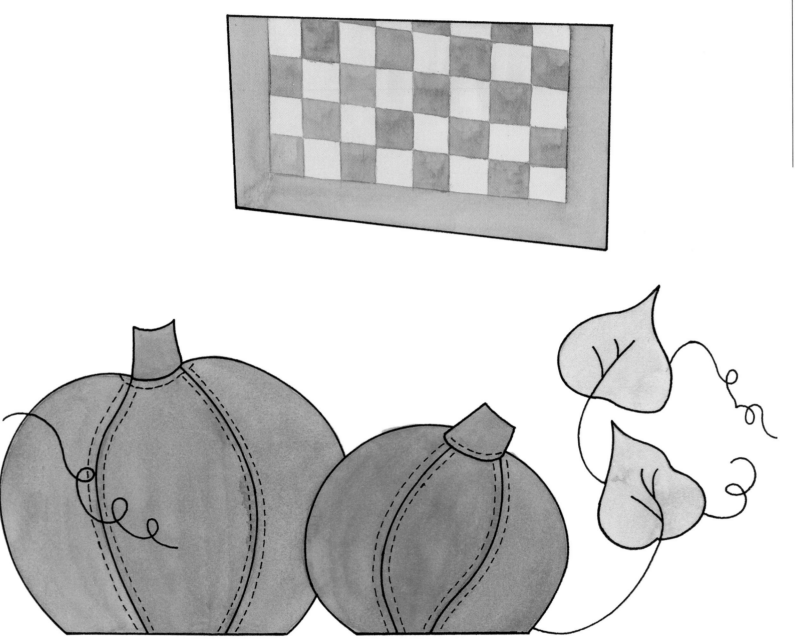

161

COUNTRY
PUMPKIN PATCH

 Moderate

WALL HANGING

What You'll Need

Large Quilt

¼ yard dark brown and black print

¼ yard orange print

⅛ yard or scraps green print

⅛ yard tan plaid

⅛ yard medium brown print

¼ yard dark orange print

¼ yard dark brown print

⅝ yard backing fabric

40×20-inch piece low-loft batting

¼ yard fusible webbing

White thread

Small Quilt

¼ yard tan print

⅛ yard orange print

⅛ yard or scraps green print

⅛ yard dark brown print for checkerboard

⅛ yard orange print for checkerboard

⅜ yard dark to medium brown print

½ yard backing fabric

18×17-inch piece low-loft batting

⅛ yard fusible webbing

White thread

Green thread

Even if Halloween's not just around the corner, you can decorate your home with pumpkins. You'll learn some neat piecing techniques as you make these folk-art treasures.

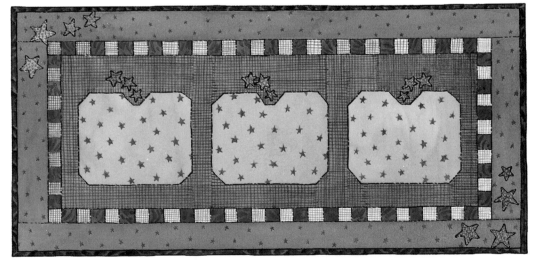

Dimensions: 38×18 inches, large quilt;
16×14½ inches, small quilt

163

For both quilts, you will use the template-free angle piecing technique. See page 49 for directions.

LARGE QUILT

1. From dark brown and black print, cut six 1-inch squares, six 1¼-inch squares, six 1½-inch squares, three 2×1½-inch rectangles, two 1½×7¼-inch rectangles, two 2×7¼-inch rectangles, one 31×1¾-inch strip, and one 31×3½-inch strip. From orange print, cut six 1-inch squares, six 4×7¼-inch rectangles, and three 2×6¼-inch rectangles. From dark orange print, cut two 3×13½-inch strips and two 3×38-inch strips. From tan and medium brown prints, cut two 1½×44-inch strips of each. From dark brown print, cut three 2½×44-inch strips.

Step 2

2. Assemble pumpkins. Using template-free angle piecing, stitch 1½-inch dark brown and black squares to upper outside corners of 4×7¼-inch orange rectangles, 1-inch dark brown and black squares to upper inside corners, and 1¼-inch squares to lower outside corners. Make 3 left sides and 3 right sides. Using template-free angle piecing, stitch two 1-inch orange squares to each 2×1½-inch dark brown and black rectangle. Make 3. Assemble 3 pumpkin blocks. Each will measure 9×7¼ inches.

3. Assemble checkerboard border. Stitch 1½×44-inch tan and medium brown strips together lengthwise, alternating colors. Press in one direction. Turn and cut into twenty-four 1½-inch units. Stitch units together end to end, alternating colors. Count off 2 rows of 31 squares each, beginning and ending with tan, and cut. Count off 2 rows of 11 squares each, beginning and ending with brown, and cut.

Step 4

4. Stitch pumpkins to 2×7¼-inch dark brown and black strips, with strips between pumpkins. Stitch 1½×7¼-inch dark brown and black strips to outer sides of pumpkin block. Stitch 31×3½-inch dark brown and black strip to top of pumpkins and 31×1¾-inch dark brown and black strip to bottom of pumpkins.

5. Stitch short checkerboard rows to each side of quilt. Press toward quilt. Stitch long checkerboard rows to top and bottom of quilt. Stitch 3×13½-inch dark orange strips to sides of quilt. Press away from quilt. Stitch 3×38-inch dark orange strips to top and bottom of quilt. Press away from quilt.

6. Trace and cut out pattern pieces on page 166. Iron fusible webbing to wrong side of green fabric. Trace 5 large stars and 12 small stars on paper side of fusible webbing, cut out, and remove paper backing. Arrange on quilt as shown in finished quilt illustration and fuse.

7. Layer front, batting, and back and baste. Using white thread, hand quilt on stars along edges. Hand quilt horizontal lines in background, curved lines in pumpkins, and star and leaf shapes in border. Hand quilt in ditches around checkerboard border. To achieve a different look and save time, you may also machine quilt. Use dark brown strips for binding. Follow directions on pages 19–20 to stitch binding to quilt.

SMALL QUILT

1. From tan print, cut twelve 1-inch squares, three 2×1-inch rectangles, one 12×1-inch strip, one 5×1-inch strip, two 4×5-inch rectangles, one 12½×2-inch strip, two 1×4½-inch rectangles, and one 2×4½-inch rectangle. From orange print, cut six 2×4½-inch rectangles, three 2×4-inch rectangles, and six 1-inch squares. From orange and dark brown prints for checkerboard, cut two 1×44-inch strips of each. From medium brown, cut two 2×12-inch strips, two 2×15½-inch strips, and two 2½×44-inch strips.

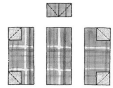

Step 2

2. Using template-free angle piecing technique, stitch 1-inch tan squares to corners of 2×4½-inch orange pieces. Make 3 right sides and 3 left sides. Stitch two 1-inch orange squares to each 2×1-inch tan piece. Make 3 units. Assemble pumpkin blocks. Each pumpkin will measure 5×4½ inches.

3. Assemble checkerboard borders, following directions for large quilt checkerboard, but make 2 rows of 23 squares beginning and ending with light and 2 rows of 21 squares beginning and ending with dark.

Step 4

4. Stitch 5×1-inch tan strip to top of one pumpkin. Add 4×5-inch tan rectangles to each side. Stitch 12×1-inch tan strip to top of unit. Join remaining two pumpkins with 2×4½-inch tan piece between them. Stitch 1×4½-inch tan pieces to each side and 12½×2-inch tan strip to top of unit. Join two-pumpkin unit with single-pumpkin unit.

5. Stitch small checkerboard borders to each side. Press toward quilt. Stitch long checkerboard borders to top and bottom of quilt. Press toward quilt. Stitch 2×12-inch medium brown strips to sides of quilt. Stitch 2×15½-inch medium brown strips to top and bottom.

6. Trace and cut out pattern pieces on page 166. Iron fusible webbing onto back of green fabric. Trace 8 small stars and 1 large star onto paper side of fusible webbing and cut out. Remove paper backing. Arrange on quilt as shown in finished quilt illustration and fuse.

7. Layer front, batting, and back and baste. Using white thread, hand quilt around appliqué stars. Hand quilt curved lines in pumpkins, star shapes in border, and in ditches around checker-board border. Using green thread, hand quilt shapes in background. To save time or create a different look, you may also machine quilt. Use remaining medium brown strips for binding. Follow directions on pages 19–20 to stitch binding to quilt.

GLOSSARY

appliqué: a group of techniques for stitching pieces of fabric onto the surface of background fabric to create a design

backing: the fabric used for the lining or reverse side of a quilt

basting: large running stitches used to temporarily secure layers of fabric together while they are being stitched

batting (batt): the filling between the quilt top and back

between: a short needle for hand quilting (the shorter the needle, the higher the number)

binding: strips of fabric that encase the outer edges of a quilt

block: one of many units that comprise a quilt top

borders: strips of fabric that frame the quilt top

chain piecing: a technique for stitching together units of a quilt block in assembly line fashion on the sewing machine

crosswise grain: the threads that are perpendicular to the selvages in a piece of woven fabric

even-feed walking foot: a sewing machine attachment that advances the top layer of fabric at the same rate that the feed dogs advance the bottom layer of fabric

feed dogs: the part of the sewing machine that advances fabric during stitching

freehand machine quilting: curves and intricate designs quilted by machine using a darning foot instead of a presser foot

freezer paper: plastic-coated paper that is sold in supermarkets for wrapping freezer foods, used by quilters to make disposable templates, especially for appliqué

fusible webbing: a synthetic material that melts when heat (usually an iron) is applied, bonding two layers of fabric or other material together

grain: the lengthwise and crosswise thread of woven fabric

paper piecing: a technique for sewing pieces of fabric together on a paper foundation that stabilizes the fabric

pin baste: to secure layers of fabric together temporarily with safety pins in preparation for stitching, usually by machine

presser foot: the part of the sewing machine that applies pressure to the fabric so that the feed dogs can advance the fabric during stitching

rotary cutter: a tool that looks and works like a pizza cutter for cutting multiple layers of fabric

quilting frame: a large plastic or wooden frame that supports a quilt during hand quilting

quilting hoop: a circular, oval, or rectangular frame that keeps a small portion of a quilt smooth for hand quilting

sashing: strips of fabric separating blocks in a quilt top

seam allowance: the narrow strip of fabric (usually ¼ inch in quilting) between the seam and the raw edges

see-through ruler: an acrylic ruler with markings for use with a rotary cutter

self-healing mat: a mat for use with a rotary cutter

selvage: the edge of woven fabric that does not fray but should always be trimmed before the fabric is used (selvages shrink more than the rest of the fabric)

sharps: general purpose hand-sewing needles used for hand piecing, appliqué, and basting

straight of grain: the lengthwise thread of woven fabric

strip piecing: a technique in which strips of fabric are cut, sewn, cut across seam lines to make units, and resewn

templates: cardboard or plastic guides for marking and cutting out pieces of fabric for piecing and appliqué and for marking quilting patterns